GUITAR WORLD PRESENTS

VAN HALEN

GUITAR WORLD PRESENTS

METALLICA

FROM THE PAGES OF

MAGAZINE

Backbeat
Books

Published in 2010 by Backbeat Books
An Imprint of Globe Pequot
4501 Forbes Boulevard, Suite 200
Lanham, Maryland 20706

Distributed by NATIONAL BOOK NETWORK

Executive Producer: Brad Tolinski
Editors: Jeff Kitts, Brad Tolinski, Chris Scapelliti
Art Director: Alexis Cook
Photo Editors: Jimmy Hubbard, Samantha Xu
Cover Photograph: Ross Halfin

Library of Congress Cataloging-in-Publication data is available upon request.

ISBN 978-0-87930-969-5

www.rowman.com

CONTENTS

GUITAR WORLD PRESENTS

VAN HALEN

[1]

"I'd rather bomb with
my own songs
than make it with someone else's."

—*EDDIE VAN HALEN*

ATOMIC PUNK

The story of how Eddie Van Halen
revolutionized rock guitar.

BY DAN AMRICH

SOME SOUNDS ARE unmistakable. Some are undefinable. More often than not, Van Halen is both.

Now, 25 years after catching the world's ear and shaking it violently, the aftershocks of Edward Van Halen's explosive guitar technique, radical ideas and boundless energy are still being felt. Surviving disco, punk, power pop, grunge and countless other trends, Eddie has proven himself as the ultimate—if somewhat reluctant—rock guitar hero.

Edward Lodewijk Van Halen was born on January 26, 1957, in Nijmegen, Holland. He and his elder brother Alex moved with their musician parents to Pasadena, California, when he was 10 years old. The family had 15 dollars and a piano, and what little of the former

Editor's note: This article contains passages that appear elsewhere in this book.

the family had went into teaching the children how to play the latter. But while Eddie respected the instrument, learned a lot about music in general and won numerous awards for his keyboard prowess, his heart wasn't in it. "Who wanted to sit at the piano?" he later said. "I wanted to go crazy!"

As American teens, Alex and Eddie learned both the English language and the language of rock and roll. Eddie invested in drums and Alex got a nylon-string acoustic guitar; while Eddie was busy delivering papers to pay for his kit, Alex was busy using it. Once Alex mastered "Wipeout," Eddie told Alex to keep the drums; he'd take the guitar. Both parties were happy. As Alex later recalled, "I could tell by the way he was moving his fingers around that he could do things I'd never be able to do, no matter how hard I practiced."

What he did with that guitar ultimately changed the face of rock, but in the early days, it was essentially just a case of jamming with his brother (using a Tiesco Del Rey electric guitar from Sears) and listening to a lot of early Beatles, Dave Clark Five, Jimi Hendrix, Jimmy Page and especially Eric Clapton, whose licks he learned note for note. Eventually, Eddie and Alex played covers at high school events with an endless stream of temporary bassists, under the name Mammoth—"a junior Cream," said Eddie. Yet the more he played, the more he realized he wanted to take his playing to the next level, beyond mere mimicry and into innovation.

But before anyone could hear Eddie's ideas, some basic problems had to be solved: primarily, finding a place to practice and finding cash to pay for a P.A. system during live gigs. Both were solved when David Lee Roth joined the band; the Van Halens had been renting Roth's equipment occasionally, and Roth's dad let them practice in the basement. The fact that Roth's extroverted antics garnered the band a lot of attention didn't hurt. When Michael Anthony gave up his own band, Snake, to play bass for Mammoth in 1974, the group became the hottest ticket in Pasadena. It wasn't too long after that they realized that Mammoth was the name of another band in the area, so Roth suggested they be known as simply Van Halen. "It had power to it," he said. Nobody could come up with anything better, so it stuck.

Playing mostly covers for five hours a night at various Southern California clubs, Eddie's technique inevitably mutated and, before long, local guitarists were heading to shows to check out his raw sound, homemade guitars and unorthodox technique of using two hands on the fretboard. Eddie, meanwhile, took his brother's advice and played solos with his back to the audience, so nobody could rip him off. As time wore on, the band got better gigs, working at legendary L.A. clubs like the Whisky and the Starwood, added more and more original material and, in 1977, caught the ear of Kiss bassist Gene Simmons. Simmons was impressed from note one and helped the band—then calling itself Daddy Longlegs—record a professional demo which was promptly rejected by every major label. It wasn't until Warner Bros. producer Ted Templeman personally convinced the label's president, Mo Ostin, to go see a VH show that the band got signed.

In February 1978, Van Halen's Templeman-produced, self-titled first album was released. An unholy wail of car horns assaulted listeners as "Runnin' with the Devil" kicked off the record, but it was merely a warning shot; the following track, "Eruption," was nothing less than pure rock guitar revolution. Pinch harmonics, hammer-ons, two-handed tapping, whammy bar dives so deep they'll give you the bends—all in one terrifying package. As the guitar world scratched its collective head and tried to figure out what the hell had just happened, Edward Van Halen had altered the very perception of what rock guitar was—in one minute, 42 seconds flat.

On the combined strengths of "Runnin' with the Devil," a high-octane cover of the Kinks' "You Really Got Me" and Ed's jaw-dropping calisthenics, *Van Halen* cracked the Top 20 and sold two million copies in a matter of months. Opening nationwide tours for acts like Montrose and Journey, the band quickly cemented a backstage reputation of babes, booze and bad behavior, spearheaded in no small part by Roth. Onstage, however, Van Halen was all business, pounding out adrenaline-soaked half-hour sets to stunned audiences. By the time they opened for Black Sabbath in Europe, the changing of the heavy rock guard was evident. "They blew us off the stage every night," recalled Ozzy Osbourne. "It was so embarrassing. We didn't have the fire anymore. They kicked our asses, but it convinced me of two things: my days with Black Sabbath were over, and Van Halen was going to be a very successful band."

By that December, the band had recorded a second album, cleverly titled *Van Halen II*. "Dance the Night Away" hit Number 15, holding its own against the disco fare of the time and, by June 1979, the band was the headline act of a U.K. tour, with 22 tons of equipment in tow. Songs like "Beautiful Girls" helped solidify David Lee Roth's party persona, while the nylon-string solo "Spanish Fly" was Eddie's proof that daring moves need not be performed on an electric.

By 1980, Van Halen had helped fuel a heavy metal resurgence—though Eddie was uncomfortable with the phrase "heavy metal" to characterize the band. David Lee Roth, meanwhile, described Van Halen's music as "a cross between religion and hockey." Still, the group's third album, *Women and Children First*, oozed distorted riffs and thundering drums, ultimately hitting number nine on the *Billboard* album chart. It also contained decidedly non-metallic gems like the acoustic slide number "Could This Be Magic?" previous to which Eddie had never played slide guitar.

While on that year's "Invasion" tour, Eddie met TV actress Valerie Bertinelli and their romance blossomed quickly; the two were married in April 1981. It's ironic, then, that in the wake of one of Eddie's happiest moments, the band released its darkest album, *Fair Warning*. Creepy synth-driven pieces like "Sunday Afternoon in the Park" and the sordid subject matter of "Mean Street" and "Dirty Movies" ultimately overshadowed party rockers like "Unchained" and "So This Is Love?" But despite Warner Bros.' decision to not release a single, the album still charted higher than any of its predecessors, reaching number six.

Bending to record company pressures, the band recorded their fifth album, *Diver Down*, in 12 days to meet an April 1982 release date. The record clocked in at under 30 minutes and contained five cover tunes within its 12 tracks, a fact that didn't sit well with Eddie. "That's my least favorite record," he said later. "I'd rather bomb with my own songs than make it with someone else's." Still, the album isn't without its gems, particularly the volume-knob trickery of "Cathedral," the Spanish-style intro to "Little Guitars" and the guest appearance of Eddie and Alex's dad, Jan Van Halen, playing clarinet on "Big Bad Bill (Is Sweet William Now)." Warner Bros. was no doubt happy, as the album soared to number three and the "Hide Your Sheep" tour kicked off at the mammoth 1982 US Festival in California.

But the tour was short and Eddie found himself with some welcome downtime at home. Unexpectedly, producer Quincy Jones called up and asked Eddie to contribute a solo to a new song for Michael Jackson's upcoming album, *Thriller*. It was generally frowned upon for Van Halen members to work outside of the band (although Eddie had previously contributed to Nicolette Larson's *Nicolette* and Brian May's *Star Fleet Project*), but since his bandmates were all out on various vacations, Eddie agreed. After requesting a different section of the song to solo over, Ed cut two takes in 20 minutes. "Beat It" spent three weeks at Number One and, largely due to Eddie's solo, crossed over to radio stations that normally wouldn't play R&B artists. *Thriller* went on to be the biggest-selling album of all time; Eddie, meanwhile, received a thank-you note and no payment, having done the solo as a favor.

While Roth later sniffed that "I ain't heard anything different," the "Beat It" favor was ultimately returned by listeners when *1984* was released on New Year's Eve, 1983. The leadoff single, "Jump," hit Number One in late February and stayed there for five weeks—to date, it's the band's only chart-topping hit. The fact that the guitar god's biggest hit was driven by a synthesizer hook seemed to bother everyone but Eddie; to him, it was just music. After all, the guy *did* have a classical piano background. Besides, the guitar faithful were rewarded with *1984*'s "Panama," "Top Jimmy" and the raucous "Hot for Teacher."

But widespread pop success came with a price. While David Lee Roth lapped up the attention, Eddie was thinking ahead to the next record. Roth had always preferred life on the road to life in a soundbooth and eventually their personal and work ethic differences came to a head. Roth had tasted solo success with his *Crazy from the Heat* album and, by June 1985, announced he was leaving the band. Ted Templeman went with him, leaving the producing duties to longtime engineer Donn Landee and the increasingly involved Eddie.

As a replacement for the acrimoniously departed Roth, the band considered doing the next album with a different lead singer on every track, but abandoned the idea after auditioning Sammy Hagar, ex-Montrose vocalist and solo artist in his own right. Hagar's fresh energy and more agreeable personality fueled 1986's *5150*, produced by Landee, the band and Mick Jones. Despite open skepticism over the missing Roth, the album became the band's first Number One record, spawning two keyboard-heavy hits, "Why Can't This Be Love" and "Dreams" as well as strong guitar rockers like "Best of Both Worlds" and some wild Steinberger antics on "Get Up." Eddie later referred to it as "a very inspired record" with "a lot of soul."

Two years of vacation later, the band headlined the Monsters of Rock tour in the summer of 1988, playing all-day concerts alongside Metallica and the Scorpions, and released the second Hagar-fronted record, *OU812*, in June. With fans eager for new material, it captured the top spot on the album charts in under a month, sitting there for four weeks. "When It's Love," "Finish What Ya Started" and "Feels So Good" all enjoyed heavy radio airplay.

After the grueling tour, the band enjoyed some well-earned R&R. In 1990, the band opened their own club, the Cabo Wabo Cantina, in Cabo San Lucas, Mexico. The next year, on March 16, 1991, Eddie and Valerie gave birth to their first son, Wolfgang William Van Halen. With another partner, Eddie soon gave birth to another child: the Ernie Ball Music Man guitar he helped design. For a tinkerer like Eddie, creating a production instrument was the ultimate thrill. "I used to endorse the guitar I played," he said, "but I designed this one. It's a whole different ballgame."

Following closely behind the new ax came a new Andy Johns–produced album, *For Unlawful Carnal Knowledge*, in June 1991. The lead single, "Poundcake," continued Ed's tradition of making weird noises with guitars thanks to its electric drill opening hook while "Top of the World" picks up where "Jump" left off—literally, as it uses the "Jump" outro as its opening riff. Although the piano-based "Right Now" turned into a huge hit, the album seemed more guitar-oriented than recent efforts, staying at the number one spot on the album charts for three weeks.

Although Eddie had said in 1985 that he "didn't see the purpose" of a live album, he eventually changed his mind for *Right Here, Right*

Now, released in February 1993. The band's first two-CD set featured material from the latest tour, a bass solo, a drum solo, lots of stage chatter from Hagar and a live solo by Eddie that encompasses "Eruption," "Cathedral," "316" and countless wild squeals. The album also featured Eddie's new Peavey 5150 amplifiers.

By the end of 1994, Eddie had severed his ties with Music Man, opting instead to evolve his earlier design for his amp manufacturer as the Peavey Wolfgang. More importantly, Eddie had stopped drinking and found that writing was far easier when he was sober. The appropriately named *Balance* debuted in January of the following year, ranging from the commercially poppy "Can't Stop Lovin' You" to the power boogie of "Big Fat Money" and no less than three instrumentals, reportedly due to difficulty getting Hagar to write lyrics. The album continued the band's Number One streak, holding the top spot for a week.

But within six months, Hagar would be history, leaving the group following disputes over the planned greatest-hits albums and the band's contributions to the *Twister* soundtrack (neatly summed up as "creative differences"). "We actually had problems on every album except for *5150*," Eddie revealed later. With Hagar's departure, old-school fans hoped beyond hope that a reunion with David Lee Roth was in the future—and it was, albeit for just two new songs for 1996's *Best of Volume 1*, "Me Wise Magic" and "Can't Get This Stuff No More." With "Magic" as its single, *Best Of* nailed *Billboard*'s top album spot, but almost as soon as the original lineup started feeling each other out, a disastrous backstage ego flareup at the MTV Video Music Awards squelched all hopes of future involvements between the band and Roth. "I'll put it very simply," said Eddie. "Dave and Sam both suffer from L.S.D.—lead singer's disease.

"Gary's very talented, and we work very, very well together," said Eddie of Van Halen's third singer, former Extreme vocalist Gary Cherone.

With Cherone on board, *Van Halen III* was, as its title suggests, a new beginning for the band, and a major milestone—the first track was called "Neuworld" for a reason. Liberated from drugs, alcohol and various other physical and mental restraints, Eddie spoke in interviews passionately about his muse, his new approach to writing and recording music, as well as his emotional and spiritual rebirth. Featuring Ed on six-string bass as well as electric sitar, the experimental album was released in February 1998, debuting at Number Four on the album charts and powered by the single "Without You." However, many fans disliked the band's new direction and the album stalled.

Dark times for Van Halen quickly followed. Almost everything that could go wrong for Eddie did. The band parted ways with Cherone in November 1999. "I had a great time singing with the band and I wish Eddie, Alex and Michael all the best," said Cherone in a statement. The band had been working on a new album with producers Patrick Leonard and Danny Kortchmar; the results of those sessions will likely never see release.

By May 2000, rumors were flying that Eddie, a longtime smoker, was battling tongue cancer. Close to a year later, Van Halen confirmed the rumors on the band's web site. "I'm sorry for having waited so long to address this issue personally, but cancer can be a very unique and private matter to deal with. I was examined by three oncologists and three head and neck surgeons at Cedars Sinai just before spring break and I was told that I'm healthier than ever and beating cancer. Although it's hard to say when, there's a good chance I will be cancer-free in the near future. I just want to thank all of you for your concern and support. Love, Eddie." By May 2002, Ed reported that he'd "gotten a 100-percent clean bill of health—from head to toe"—but his 21-year marriage to Valerie Bertinelli was not so lucky, ultimately ending in July 2002. To make matters worse, Warner Bros. very quietly had dropped the band from its artist roster some months earlier. After more than 70 million albums sold worldwide, one of the all-time great rock and roll bands found itself homeless.

Then, impossibly, David Lee Roth and Sammy Hagar joined forces for a tour together in the summer of 2002. Humbly titled Song for Song: The Heavyweight Champs of Rock and Roll Tour (but nicknamed the "Sans Halen" tour by fans), Sam and Dave played dates through September, with Dave dipping into the classic VH catalog more often than Sammy. "I'm not sure what the [Van Halen] brothers think, and I'm not sure I even really care," said Roth during the press blitz. "I think probably the two biggest words up there on Howdy Doody mountain now are 'Uh-oh.'" Dave's subsequent filing and dropping of a lawsuit against his former bandmates later in the year only seemed to dash hopes of an eventual reunion.

Sammy, however, sent mixed messages over the course of the summer, saying "Quite honestly, I'm not interested" to the Wisconsin *Journal Sentinel* in June but "I think a reunion is inevitable" at the MTV Video Music Awards three months later. Sure enough, by the fall of 2003, reunion rumors once again circulated, this time with Sammy at the lead, but the Van Halen camp kept silent, until finally announcing tour dates and a new band photo in March 2004. The tour was in support of a *Best of Volume 2*, spearheaded by the appropriately titled Sammy-sung single, "It's About Time."

World tours, roster changes, life-threatening illnesses, David Lee Roth—Van Halen, it seems, can survive anything. Having passed the 25-year mark, the band is less a mere musical group and more a simple force of nature: unpredictable, indestructible and undeniably powerful. At age 47, Eddie remains what he has always been: a master guitarist, supremely confident of his craft and his multiple role as songwriter, producer and musician. "I still have so much music in me," says Eddie. "So much that needs to come out."

REPRINTED FROM *GUITAR WORLD*, APRIL 2008

[2]

A new movement was taking place and Van Halen, with a bratty authority and a rapacious sense of purpose not heard since the debut of Led Zeppelin, were leading the charge.

VH1

In 1978, Van Halen burst out of the Sunset Strip
and set the music world on fire with their debut
album. This is the story behind the group's rise
to success and the making of *Van Halen*, the
record that changed guitar-oriented rock forever.

BY JOE BOSSO

THIRTY YEARS AGO, Van Halen arrived when music was in desperate need of them. Belching fire and brimstone and fighting for their right to party while the Beastie Boys were still in middle school, their timing was impeccable. When *Van Halen*, the Pasadena, California–based group's debut album, was released on February 10, 1978, there were hardly any stars in American music. The album not only made celebrities of the group's four members—it also gave new life to guitar-oriented rock and made virtuosity a criterion for any guitarist who hoped to follow in the group's footsteps.

From the start, everything about Van Halen seemed to suggest grandness of scale: Their name, which, somewhat surprisingly,

Editor's note: This article contains passages that appear elsewhere in this book.

singer David Lee Roth had to convince Eddie Van Halen into using in place of the more directly size-centric Mammoth (Eddie later admitted that his surname was the perfect choice: "It sounds huge, like an atomic bomb."). Their outsized stage show, perfected at backyard keggers and wet T-shirt contests, and eventually at Sunset Strip clubs like the Whisky a Go-Go and Gazzarri's.

And, of course, their energy. Van Halen had swagger, good looks and smiles—that magical show-biz triumvirate introduced and perfected by the Beatles that had somehow become lost over the years. What's more, they and their music were fun. By the early Seventies, music was beginning to feel like work: the prog-rock movement brought staggering feats of virtuosic musicianship, but the music was full of torturous 20-minute opuses about space travel and Knights of the Round Table. Van Halen seemed to understand that music could be the antidote to cynicism, that it could make you feel alive again. "I think the thing that separated me and the rest of the band from everybody else was the fact that we just loved to play," Eddie recalled. "That's the thing: you don't *work* music, you *play* music."

There was also that sound, a ground shaker that matched the audacity of the band's ambitions. It was based on booming drums and gushers of distorted guitar, jacked up by Eddie's personally modified guitars and amplifiers (the guitarist famously used Variacs to lower the line voltage of his amps, thereby reducing headroom and causing the power tubes to compress and distort more). Rarely in the annals of rock did a sound serve a band so beautifully: the higher the volume, the larger the canvas, the more inspired the music making.

Most important, there was Eddie's singular approach to the guitar, honed at first by years of obsessively studying the styles of Hendrix, Beck and, in particular, Eric Clapton. Slowing down Cream records to copy the solos to songs such as "Spoonful" brought the young guitarist only so far. By his mid-teens, out of frustration and sheer force of will, he flipped the bird to convention and became a recluse, shutting himself in his bedroom for 12 hours at a time to devote himself to the instrument and the strange and wondrous noises he heard in his head. "I used to sit on the edge of my bed with a six-pack of Schlitz Malt talls," he said. "My brother [*Alex*] would go out at 7 P.M. to party and get laid, and when he'd come back at 3 A.M., I would still be sitting in the same place, playing guitar. I did that for years."

When he finally emerged from his room and hit the Hollywood stages with Van Halen (which included Alex on drums, Michael Anthony on bass and Roth), his breathtaking abilities were nearly fully formed, as was his unorthodox hammer-on-and-pull-off technique. Eddie readily admits that he wasn't the first guitarist to employ this approach, but the manner in which he brought it to the fore, with a commitment and finesse that transcended mere gimmickry, was seen as shocking, revolutionary and, above all, baffling. "I think I got the idea of tapping watching Jimmy Page do his 'Heartbreaker' solo back in 1971," he recalled. "He was doing a pull-off to an open string, and I thought, Wait a minute, open string...pull off. I can do that, but what if I use my finger as the nut and move it around? I just kind of took it and ran with it."

Still precocious enough to be considered an *enfant terrible*, Eddie Van Halen incited strong reactions and drew legions of fascinated (and no doubt envious) guitarists to his band's shows. When performing live in those early years, he played with his back to the audience. While this might have been seen as an act of supreme humility, as if some part of him rebelled against canonization, it was in fact an act of self-preservation. His brother Alex, demonstrating uncanny prescience, had warned him that other guitarists would "rob him blind" if his tricks were exposed before the band could cut a record. It was only after the release of *Van Halen* that Eddie, secure in the knowledge that his feats of fretboard wizardry had been sufficiently documented, felt comfortable playing facing a crowd.

But even before he tracked his first note in a professional recording studio, he was putting serious distance between himself and his peers—and his heroes. Many guitarists have a talent, but to be successful it is not enough to have talent; one must have a certain *kind* of talent. Hendrix was a shape-shifter of sound in a psychedelic, blues-based idiom. Page was a master of moods, production and arrangement. Beck was flash stylist. Clapton had tone, taste and knew his way around pop composition. With Eddie Van Halen, all of the above applied. His thing was, he could do it all. And, along with David Lee Roth, he was penning songs that were tight and tuneful—the stuff that hits are made of.

"I think I got the idea of tapping watching Jimmy Page do his 'Heartbreaker' solo back in 1971."

Their reputation for drawing audiences was built quickly. Soon the band was opening for the likes of Santana, UFO, Nils Lofgren and Sparks. When scenester and show promoter Rodney Bingenheimer booked Van Halen into the Starwood club, Kiss' Gene Simmons caught their act and was floored. Taking the Pasadena upstarts under his leathery wing, Simmons financed the band's first professional demo tape. Basics for the songs "Runnin' with the Devil" and "House of Pain" (the latter of which would appear on the album *1984*) were cut at Village Recorder Studios in Los Angeles. Later, Simmons, who was trying to persuade the band into calling themselves Daddy Longlegs (an idea they rejected out of hand), flew the group to New York to finish recording at Electric Ladyland Studios in New York.

It was there that Eddie had his first exposure with the practice of overdubbing; the guitarist was anything but comfortable with the process. "I tried to do it, but I just didn't know how," he said. "You have to play to yourself. I was like, 'How the hell do I do this?' I hadn't even played with another guitarist.' While in New York, Simmons arranged for the band to perform a showcase for Kiss' manager Bill Aucoin. Aucoin agreed with Simmons that Van Halen had spirit, but he felt their commercial prospects were limited; instead, the manager set his sights on signing a band called Piper, whose commercial prospects proved to be even less than limited. With their demo tape in hand, Van Halen headed back to California, buoyed by their brush with success but uncertain when their real break would come.

Although they were stars on the Sunset Strip, the band wasn't seeing much money; some gigs paid no more than $75. "Not even enough to buy equipment," Eddie recalled. "Alex and I used to go around and paint house numbers on curbs to make extra money." All of that changed during another Starwood performance when the band was introduced to Marshall Berle, nephew of comedian and TV icon Milton Berle, who became the group's manager. Berle had a flair for hype, but something about the way he talked up Van Halen and their ability to draw crowds led Warner Bros. head Mo Ostin to believe that maybe this was more than just talk—perhaps there was something to this band from Pasadena after all. And so, on a night that saw heavy rain flood the Hollywood streets, Van Halen played to a nearly empty Starwood. Mo

Ostin was there, along with Warner Bros. in-house producer Ted Templeman. Despite the nonexistent crowd, Van Halen played with unbridled brio. Ostin and Templeman looked at each other and smiled: They would sign the band, as in right away. "It was right out of the movies," Eddie said. "Just like that, we finally had a record deal."

Templeman, who had produced albums for Van Morrison, Carly Simon and Captain Beefheart, among others, and who enjoyed a long and fruitful association with the Doobie Brothers, was astounded by Van Halen's surfeit of strong material, and he wasted little time in hustling them into Sunset Sound Studios. Once in the studio, even less time was wasted: In only 18 days, the band raced through their entire repertoire, 40 songs in all, originals as well as covers such as the Kinks' "You Really Got Me" and John Brim's blues standard "Ice Cream Man." On the songs that didn't require a vibrato bar ("You Really Got Me," "Runnin' with the Devil," the rhythm track for "Jamie's Cryin' "), Eddie employed his main live guitar, an Ibanez "Shark" Destroyer. On other songs, he used a black-and-white striped Strat that he outfitted with a Gibson Fifties PAF humbucker.

Much to Eddie's relief, Templeman wasn't the punctilious sort; the producer was in thrall of the band's live performance qualities and insisted on keeping instrumental overdubs to a minimum. "It was a party," Eddie said of the sessions. "We played the way we played onstage, and it was great. It didn't feel like we were making a record. We just went in, poured back a few beers and played."

> "We just went in, poured back a few beers and played."

The tracks for the album had almost all been cut when, one day, Templeman walked into the studio and heard Eddie and Alex warming up for a show the band was to play that night at the Whisky. According to Eddie, the two were just "dickin' around," but Templeman sensed something else was happening, a breakthrough of some sort. He watched and listened in hypnotic excitement as the guitarist's fingers danced along the fretboard. These weren't the normal scales and patterns Eddie had traditionally practiced to limber up; these were strange and exciting song fragments, a voluptuous feast of ideas, operatic in scope but performed with a savage, erotic force. Templeman had already been telling friends and associates about this marvelous new guitarist he'd been working with, going so far as to compare him to the likes of Django Reinhardt and Andrés Segovia,

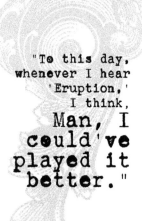

"To this day, whenever I hear 'Eruption,' I think, Man, I could've played it better."

but now he was convinced of Eddie Van Halen's genius. He asked Eddie what it was he was playing. "Oh, that's a little solo thing I do live," he responded. Templeman didn't recall Van Halen playing it at the Starwood show he attended, but he insisted that the instrumental be fleshed out and cut for the album.

In one breathless take, after a short, bombastic intro with Alex and Michael Anthony, Eddie released an unbroken ribbon of scales, bends, dive bombs and hammer-on classical-sounding arpeggios. As he did in all of the band's songs, Eddie tuned down a half step (this was done both to accommodate Roth's vocal style and to give the guitar sound more teeth). The only effects that were used were an MXR Phase 90 and a Univox EC-80 echo box (the latter of which was housed in an old WWII bomb shell that Eddie found in a junkyard). One minute and forty-two seconds after the tape started rolling, Eddie pulled his vibrato bar up after a long, descending growl and "Eruption," as it was now called, was complete. Templeman and the band were elated, but Eddie was chastened. "I didn't even play it right," he later remarked. "There's a mistake at the top end of it. To this day, whenever I hear it I always think, Man, I could've played it better."

Eddie would soon make one more screw up, only this wouldn't go down so well. With the album still months away from release, he went to the Rainbow Bar & Grill and hug out with members of a fellow Sunset Strip band called Angel. As alcohol flowed, drummer Barry Brandt began to brag about the forthcoming Angel record. Eddie, flush with pride over the album he had just cut, responded in kind. When the party moved to Brandt's house, Eddie, hell bent on blowing everybody's mind, put on a tape of *Van Halen*—and jaws were dropped. Eddie thought nothing of it—for weeks he had been playing the tape for his friends—but when he got a call from a furious Ted Templeman, informing him that Angel were in a studio frantically recording their own version of "You Really Got Me" with the intention of beating Van Halen to the punch, he realized the magnitude of his mistake. As a consequence, Warner Bros. had no choice but to rush-release Van Halen's version of the song. (It should be noted that Angel would soon join Piper in the Oblivion bins at record shops.)

There were no riots in the streets, nobody threw anything (except guitars out of windows), but it's safe to say that from the moment people dropped the needle on *Van Halen* and heard what seemed to some sort of air-raid alarm (actually, it was the band members' car horns synced together and slowed down to ominous effect) they were in a state of shock. A new movement was taking place, and Van Halen, with a bratty authority and a rapacious sense of purpose not heard since the debut of Led Zeppelin, were leading the charge. A nearly flawless piece of pop art, *Van Halen* is one of those great rarities in music, at once simple and sophisticated, distilling the band's prodigious chops and party-hearty aesthetic into hummable melodies that took hold of one's senses and didn't let go. "Ain't Talkin' 'Bout Love," "Jamie's Cryin,' " "Runnin with the Devil," "I'm on Fire"—there isn't a bum track to be found. As both singer and carnival barker of sorts, David Lee Roth made all the right noises: surprised whoops, leering come-ons, testicle-gripping screams, hollers of "whoa now" and the like—the full panoply of orchestrated let-me-entertain-you shtick. Alex Van Halen and Michael Anthony more than held up their respective ends, providing a prizefighter's punch and, in the case of Anthony, background vocals that sailed in the air and served as the perfect counterpoint to Roth's gruff voice.

Of course, there was Eddie. Of all the young guitarists who ever issued a debut record, he's the one who delivered on promises he never had to make. Dispensing with the usual wobbly preamble of a flawed but ambitious first record, he burst through the gate as a musician who valued substance and emotional contact over mere technical flash. With poetry in his heart and a panoramic vision of where he was headed, he never had to develop into something special, for he was already there. Being thrust into the pantheon of greats at such a tender age (he was 22 at the time) and so early in his career can be ruinous to most musicians, but Eddie's extraordinary energy and thirst for innovation proved to be invaluable strengths. Guitarists the world over saw the rashness and speed of his gifts and emulated him in a way that no musician has ever had to endure. "Eruption" was and continues to be a litmus test for budding ax slingers—what Frank Zappa's "The Black Page" is to drummers, so, too, Eddie's tour de force is to guitarists. But it's also a cul-de-sac, for no matter how hard everyone tried to catch up to Eddie Van Halen, he was burning up the ground as fast as he could run.

Thirty-two years on, it continues unabated.

[3]

"I wanted to be a
rock and roll star."
—EDDIE VAN HALEN

CALIFORNIA DREAMIN'

In this never-before-published interview conducted just a few weeks after the February 1978 release of *Van Halen*, Eddie Van Halen spoke out about his lifelong dreams of being a rock star.

BY STEVEN ROSEN

Lost Interview #1

GUITAR WORLD Was your father a musician?

EDDIE VAN HALEN Yeah, he got us into music very early. He got Al [*Alex Van Halen, Eddie's brother*] and me practicing piano for concert stuff, classical piano, at like seven and eight years old.

GW You were that young?

VAN HALEN Oh, yeah. My brother was six, I think, when he started and I started when I was about seven. Then my family moved [*from the Netherlands*] to southern California and we started getting into rock and roll a little bit. The Dave Clark Five, the real early stuff. And I went out and got myself a paper route and bought a drum set.

Originally I played drums and my brother played guitar.

GW Is that right?

VAN HALEN While I was out throwin' my papers, he was practicing my drums. He got better than I did and I said, "Okay, you play my drums and I'll pick up your guitar." It went on from there. I'd say I really didn't start playing guitar and getting into lead guitar and stuff like that until Cream came out; when the heavy guitar thing started to happen.

GW Do you remember the first guitar you had?

VAN HALEN Yeah. [*laughs*] A Sears Teisco Del Rey; a three-pickup job. I thought the more pickups and switches it had, the better guitar it was. Nowadays I've got kind of a homemade copy of a Strat with just one pickup and one volume knob. Really simple. It looks like a Strat but there's a place in San Dimas, California, called Charvel Guitars and they custom make 'em. Mine wasn't really custom made—it was like a junk neck and a hacked-up body that was just lying around and I wanted to experiment building my own guitar. So I could get the sound I wanted. See, I always wanted a Strat for the vibrato bar because I love that effect. So I just bought it from them for $50 and the neck for $90 and slapped it together. Put an old humbucking pickup in it and one volume knob and painted it up the way I wanted it to look and it screams. My main guitar up until right now.

GW Is that the black and white striped guitar?

VAN HALEN Yeah—it's the one on the cover of the album. Just one pickup and one volume knob—no tone or fancy out-of-phase switches or nothin' like that.

GW You used to use a Fender Strat?

VAN HALEN Yeah, but I couldn't get the sound I wanted out of a regular Strat. Somebody told me about the Charvel place and about their wood. Their bodies get much better tone and stuff like that, so I checked it out.

GW You only need the one volume control and the single pickup to get all the tone you need?

VAN HALEN Yeah. I use a couple of effects, like an MXR phase shifter, a flanger and two Echoplexes, which change the sound a bit. And I use two Univox echo boxes also for the end of my solo on "Eruption." That's not an Echoplex; it's a Univox. Everything I use is MXR; it's about all I can afford. Mounted on a piece of wood. I use a pretty long cord onstage—about a 25- or a 30-footer, and after it goes through the pedals I use an equalizer to boost the line back up. But tone-wise I just crank everything all the way up and, depending on how you pick, you get different tones and stuff. My amp setup is pretty tricked though.

GW Tell me about your rig.

VAN HALEN I've got six old Marshalls that have been rebuilt. They have bigger tubes in 'em and bigger transformers to make 'em a lot louder. I use six heads hooked to six cabinets. The cabinets are pretty much stock except I changed the way they look a little bit. And I use these things called voltage generators. What this box does is it enables me to crank up the voltage higher than the amp is supposed to take. It really makes the tubes red-hot, you know; it really makes the amp overload so much that it gets the sound I like.

GW Do you use any special settings on the Marshalls?

VAN HALEN I just crank 'em all the way up—everything all the way up.

GW Do you use the same setup in the studio?

VAN HALEN I use the exact same thing.

GW You actually crank up six Marshall stacks in the studio?

VAN HALEN Oh, no, no no. [*laughs*] Okay, see, the thing is I get the exact same sound out of one or out of six. All the difference in numbers just means how loud it's gonna be. And each amp sounds the same. I use two actually because I like to feel it too while I'm playing.

GW It must be pretty loud in the studio.

VAN HALEN Oh, yeah—we play at stage volume. We recorded at Sunset Sound...I like that room. It's just a big room—it's like our basement, actually. The guys who run the studio and maintain the place, they walk in after we're done, and there are beer cans all over the floor and Pink's hot dog smears all over the place. But in order for us to be comfortable we just do what we want.

GW How you do you manage to keep your guitar in tune with so much whammy bar stuff going on in your playing?

VAN HALEN That is a very tricky question. So far I haven't told or showed anybody. I dicked around with a Strat for years learning how to do that and there's about four or five different things that you have to do, including knowing the technique of playing it. A lot of people just grab the bar and go wahwahwahwahwah [*mimics the sound of a bar going up and down*] and expect it to stay in tune. There are little things that you have to do, like after you hit the bar and you bring the note down, usually one of the strings goes sharp. So before you come back in with a full chord, you have to stretch with your left hand to pop it back. Without picking the string, you just grab the string and jerk it up real quick and then it pops right back to where it was before you hit the bar. And then on top of that, you know the little metal jobs at the top? What part of the guitar is that? I don't even know. Where the tuning pegs are, Fender always has these little metal things that hold the strings down. String retainers or whatever they're called. If you have those too tight, the string will get caught up on that and it won't pop back the way it's supposed to. Also, it's the way you wind your strings.

GW How do you wind your strings?

VAN HALEN Hey, I don't know if I want to tell you! It's basically simple and the kind of strings you use is important. I use Fender strings—they're very good and I like 'em.

GW What gauges do you use?

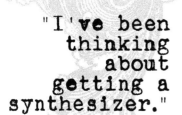

"I've been thinking about getting a synthesizer."

VAN HALEN They're pretty light, really: .040, .032, .024, .015, .011 and .009. So far for that Strat those are the best gauges for keeping it in tune. I used to think that the heavier strings I used, the better it would stay in tune, but that ain't true either.

GW Have you done anything to the tuning pegs themselves?

VAN HALEN I use Schallers—they're not regular Fenders.

GW Have you played with the bridge?

VAN HALEN The spring setup—they come with five springs and I only use four. It's hard to explain everything because it also depends on the guitar. I could tell you exactly what to do and you could do it to your Strat and it wouldn't work. And also there's a thing in the back where the strings hook up; there are two long screws and how tight you got that set, it changes the tension of the springs. So it's that—how you wind your strings, how many springs you got, the string retainers at the top and the way you play it. It took me a while to figure it out.

GW Do you think you'll stick with these Strat-styled guitars?

VAN HALEN When we were in New Orleans, I just bought a Les Paul. I needed another guitar because I tend to bend the hell out of the strings a lot—usually after my solo live, I change guitars. So I needed another guitar and when we were in New Orleans I just picked up a Les Paul. It's a real nice white one.

GW Do you play any acoustic guitar?

VAN HALEN I have never in my life owned an acoustic guitar; I really haven't. I've written songs on electric guitar that would sound real nice on an acoustic but I've never owned an acoustic guitar. I guess one of these days I'll buy one. I don't know anything about acoustics. I know what I like in electric guitars, but acoustic I'm lost. I don't know what's good.

GW Do you play any slide guitar?

VAN HALEN A little bit; there's nothing on the record. There's no slide on the record. But who knows what lurks in the future? Me and my brother both play keyboards, too—I've been thinking about getting a synthesizer. But who knows? I might not.

GW Do you use any special tunings?

VAN HALEN Sometimes I bring the low E down to a D for some acoustic stuff; it sounds real deep.

GW What about picks?

VAN HALEN Fender mediums. What I used to do was use a metal pick. A friend of mine worked in a machine shop and he always used to make me metal picks. And they were really cool—but hard to hold onto when you start sweating. They'd fly out of my hand and I'd be bummed out.

GW Can you talk about how you developed that fast, fluttering pick attack?

VAN HALEN Just practice, I guess. I've been playing eight to 10 years; that's quite a while. I kind of pick at a downward angle. And I started early, which is good. A lot of people start late and play for 10 years and they don't get quite as far. I enjoy playing—that's the main thing. It's not like I was forcing myself. I wanted to be a rock and roll star. I started out playing because I really liked to.

GW Do you still practice?

VAN HALEN Sure. I mean, I've got a guitar right here in my hands right now. I change the strings before a gig; I play for half-an-hour, an hour, just to break in the strings and loosen up my fingers. And at night sometimes I come home and write a tune.

GW You change the strings before every gig?

VAN HALEN Oh, yeah, every day—especially on the Strat; they wear out so quick with that bar.

GW Talking about the album, it really sounds like there isn't a lot of overdubbing going on.

VAN HALEN Oh, no, no. I hate overdubbing because it's just not the same as playing with the guys—there's no feeling there for me to work off of. I've got to feed off them to play good, too. Like "Runnin' with the Devil" is a melodic solo, so I put a rhythm underneath it. Songs that have a spontaneous solo, like "I'm the One," "Ice Cream Man" and most of the songs on the album, Ted Templeman, our producer, felt that it was good enough on its own without fattening it up. Also, when we play it live, it sounds the same. I don't like it when bands over-produce in the studio and then when they play live it doesn't sound the same. With us it sounds exactly the same and maybe even better because you get to see us doing it at the same time. It's very energetic—we'll get you up and shake your ass.

GW Was Ted important in bringing out the best in you?

VAN HALEN Oh, sure. What he managed to do was put our live sound on a record. I mean, a lot of people have to do a bunch of overdubs to make it sound full. It's a lot easier to make a lot of instruments sound full than a guitar, bass and drums. That's where Ted comes in—he knows his shit. He's the man. He's doing our next one, too.

GW You were pleased with your solos and the sound of your guitar on *Van Halen*?

VAN HALEN It was cool. I'm not saying I couldn't do better, but for a first album it only took us a week just to do the music. Everything was basically done in a first or second take.

GW Any solos that stand out for you?

VAN HALEN I don't know. I like all the songs and I like all the solos. I guess it takes someone from the outside to pick which one they like best. I really like the solo in "I'm the One," the boogie. That one was pretty much spontaneous—whereas "Runnin' with the Devil" and "On Fire" and some of the other ones were set solos. But "I'm the One" gave me a chance to space off a little bit and noodle around. Which I do a lot live; we all get crazy live. I mean, nobody spaces off to the point where it falls apart; we just add a little bit visually and sound-wise but keep it interesting.

GW Are there certain scales and things that you work from in putting together your solos?

VAN HALEN Truth is I don't really know what scales they are. [*laughs*] I really don't. I know music theory and I know how to write music on paper and how to read for piano, but on guitar it's a different story. I don't know nothin' about what a scale is; I know basic notes. I can play what sounds good—what I think is good, anyway.

GW I hear a Ritchie Blackmore influence in your playing.

VAN HALEN Since the last five or six years, I really haven't been into any one guitarist—I like everybody. I've listened to Blackmore and Jeff Beck—especially Beck's *Wired*, I like some of that stuff. Before that I just never really got into him. I didn't like him with Beck, Bogert & Appice. But the main guitarist I'd say that influenced me to play the most was Eric Clapton. I used to love the way he played—he was real smooth and had a lot of feeling. Every review I ever read of our album or my playing it's always about the Blackmore, Beck and Page influence. But I never really sat down and copped their licks like I did Clapton. I guess a lot of people think I sound like Beck or Blackmore because I do use the bar and they do also, so it kinda gets the same sound. The only thing Blackmore got me hooked on was the whammy bar. Because I never really liked the way he played that weird staccato stuff. But I feel a lot of my licks are different than theirs. Like the wide stretch things I do I try and make it sound a little bit different.

GW You do that one thing during "Eruption" where you're hitting a note and...

VAN HALEN Right, right—it's like having a sixth finger on your left hand. Instead of picking you're hitting a note on the fretboard.

GW Was this a technique that you developed or was it just something you stumbled across?

VAN HALEN I really don't know how to explain that. I was just sitting in my room at home, drinkin' a beer, and I remembered seeing people stretching one note and hitting the note once. They popped the finger on there to hit one note. I said, "Well, nobody is really capitalizing on that. Nobody was really doing more than just one stretch and one note real quick." So I started dickin' around and said, "Fuck! This is another technique that nobody really does!" Which it is. I haven't really seen anyone get into that as far as they could because it is a totally different sound. A lot of people listen to that and they don't even think it's a guitar. "Is that a synthesizer? A piano? What is that?"

GW The way you hit harmonics at the beginning of some of the songs from the album also sound different than the way other guitarists hit them.

VAN HALEN I just liked the sound of it and I just kept workin' at it until I got the notes I wanted. You can almost do a complete scale with all the harmonics. Just gotta know where to him 'em. I guess I could be funny and say I take a lot of pills, but that ain't true.

GW Did you have any idea that the band would have such success? You're out touring with Montrose and Journey and you're going to Japan in March. That must feel amazing.

VAN HALEN We're all trippin' on that it happened quick. We've been together for four years as a band. I talk to these guys in Journey and they go, "Wow, man, you guys are lucky because it happened so quick for you." But what they don't understand is we'd been together for four years before the album got out.

GW How were you able to promote Van Halen in the early days?

VAN HALEN A lot of bands make a demo tape; we did that also. We went to New York with Gene Simmons from Kiss around two years ago. He saw us in a club and asked us, "Are you guys on a label or anything? Do you have a manager?" and we said, "No." So he said, "Wow, you guys are a hot band, I'd like to work with you guys." And we're going, "What do you mean?" And what it boiled down to was he wanted to take a shot at producing a rock band so we said "Sure," because he was payin' for it all. We didn't have any money and I guess basically that's why we did the tape. But then again we went to New York, made the world's most expensive demo tape, and never ended up using it. On top of not having a tape, we didn't know where in the hell to take it; we didn't know anyone.

Bands usually just take it to a record company and where some clown sittin' on a couch and smokin' a joint listens to your tape, and nothing

"All we're tryin'
to do is
**put some
excitement
back into
rock and
roll.**"

will ever happen that way. So what we basically did was just kept playing the L.A. area everywhere. We used to put on our own shows in our hometown and draw like 3,000 people on a $4 ticket. This was way before Warner Bros. So we just developed a following that way, and the word got out.

GW Then you had some people from Warner Bros. come down and see the band?

VAN HALEN Finally Ted Templeman and Mo Ostin came down to the Starwood in Hollywood, which was always kind of a bad place for us because we weren't a Hollywood band. Where we're from in Pasadena is really not like Hollywood at all. Anyway, it really tripped me out because when we were playin' and Mo Ostin and Ted Templeman walked in, we really didn't know. Somebody just said, "There's somebody real important out there, so play good." It was just a rainy Monday night, and there was hardly anyone in the crowd. And still Mo and Ted came backstage and said they loved it. They said, "If you don't negotiate with anyone else, you've got what you want right here." We were happy—we tripped out. Warner Bros., man, that was always the company I wanted to be with. On top of that, we got Ted Templeman to produce the record.

I talked to a lot of people who we've played with and they say, "Wow, man, we're trying to get Ted Templeman to produce our record." He's in demand and here we are, we get picked up by him.

GW Have you written any songs for the next album?

VAN HALEN Oh, yeah, we write all the time. That's a good thing about the band—everybody contributes. I'm the guitarist, so I write all the riffs and shit but Dave [*Lee Roth*] writes lyrics and Al and Mike

[*Anthony*] really help arrange; every song is a group effort. There's not one song that one person wrote totally.

GW Who's idea was it to release "You Really Got Me" as the first single?

VAN HALEN It was a joint effort between us and Ted. The night he saw us play we played that song and he got off on it. He's going, "Hey, man, that might be a good song to put on the record." We've all been waiting to do that song anyways since we were four years old. I mean, it sounds different than the original—it's kind of updated. Van Halen–ized like a jet plane.

GW How has the record been selling?

VAN HALEN Pretty good—we've sold about 350,000. We're like 29 with a bullet next week in *Billboard*. So we're kickin' some ass. When we started out with Journey and Montrose, we were brand new; I think our album was only out a week at the start of the tour. And now we're almost passing up Journey on the charts and stuff. So they're freakin'out. I think they might be happy to get rid of us. We're very energetic and we get up there and blaze on the people for 30 minutes—that's all we're allowed to play with them. They won't let us use any effects. For my solo, "Eruption," I do that every night live and I have this old World War II bomb which is about six or seven feet tall and I put some echo boxes in it. Usually the thing blows up at the end of my solo with all the smoke bombs, but they won't let me use it. We don't get soundchecks; we don't get shit. But we're still blazin' on the people, man—we're getting a good strong encore every night.

All we're tryin' to do is put some excitement back into rock and roll. It seems like a lot of people are old enough to be our daddies and they sound like it or they act like it—they seem energy-less. It seems like they forget what rock and roll is all about.

[4]

"Sometimes you start thinking so much that you blow it."
—EDDIE VAN HALEN

BOTTOMS UP!

Their 1979 New Year's Eve gig may have been
canceled due to David Lee Roth's broken foot, but
that didn't keep Van Halen from partying it up
during the recording of *Van Halen II*.

BY STEVEN ROSEN

Lost Interview #2

GUITAR WORLD When did you start working on the second album?

EDDIE VAN HALEN We started on the Monday after our last gig—we jumped in right away because we figured we might as well get it out of the way. That was about two weeks ago. We were obviously a lot tighter than if we took a couple weeks off and partied it up every weekend. So Ted [*Templeman, producer*] suggested it and we said, "Yeah, we were gonna ask you if we could do it right away." We were much tighter because we'd just played for 10 straight months. Even if you're half asleep there's something there—you're just tight without knowing it. We went in Monday and Tuesday we rehearsed—Wednesday and

Thursday we recorded about four or five songs. And then we took off because we had to write some more songs.

GW You didn't have the album already written?

VAN HALEN No, not at all actually.

GW Did you think the first album would have done as well as it did?

VAN HALEN Hell no! Who knows? The next one might bomb. [*laughs*] I feel pretty good about this one; the first one I had no idea. Even though we took the same approach on this one. We just do what we come up with as opposed to forcing ourselves to write something commercial. Some of the stuff will probably never get any airplay. But that's what I really like—I get off on playing that stuff. I like the hard stuff.

GW Did you take what you learned on the first album and apply it to this one?

VAN HALEN It was actually exactly like the first record—we just set up in a big room. I used almost everything I used onstage, only I used my old Marshalls as opposed to brand new ones that I use onstage. I don't like using the old ones onstage because I've lost 'em before and they sound, to my ear, so good. I put them in a closet and leave them there.

GW So there wasn't much overdubbing this time either?

VAN HALEN Oh, not at all. There will be 10 songs on the album and three of them have guitar overdubs. The rest are live.

GW What's the album called?

VAN HALEN *Van Halen...*

GW *...Two?*

VAN HALEN Yeah. I didn't say it, you said it. No, it's just gonna have the logo on the front and on top where it says Van Halen it'll say *Van Halen II* just so the audience will know it's not the first one—it's the second one. But we don't mean to bill it as *Van Halen II* or like *Queen II*.

" **That kinda pissed me off** about the first album—that there wasn't enough drums. "

GW You didn't consciously try to write the types of songs that were on the first album? You didn't write another "Runnin' with the Devil"?

VAN HALEN No. The songs aren't at all the same. Well, the first album too we didn't consciously write "Devil." It just came out that way. It wasn't like, "Hey, we need a song with the bass going *bomp bomp bomp* [*mimics opening lick*]. It's just the way it happened. I'm real happy with this record because it still sounds like Van Halen, which is three instruments and voices with very few overdubs and very live sounding. As opposed to other bands—without mentioning any names—who do try and re-do their first album. They think, Oh, wow, we hit it with that one and we've got to follow the same format. Which we didn't do at all. When the record comes out and it's all sequenced, I bet it won't be at all like the first one.

GW How would you describe the sound of the album?

VAN HALEN It's just much fuller. Also Ted and Donn Landee, the engineer, for the first record they weren't quite sure of what we wanted and they weren't too familiar with our sound and now they are. So I guess it's just growing. We play better, we write better, and they in turn know how to bring the sound out better for us. Ted said when we rehearsed, "God, I can't believe how tight you guys are compared to the first record."

GW Can you give me a rundown of the songs?

VAN HALEN I can't even remember the songs. I can go out and get the tape. [*Edward runs outside and retrieves the cassette from his car* *stereo.*] Okay, the first song on the tape is "Outta Love Again," which sounds like [*Tower of Power's*] "What Is Hip." It sounds more funky. Everyone can relate to that; everyone falls in love and out of love. I really like that song because it makes the drums shine. That kinda pissed me off about the first record—that there wasn't enough drums. On this album there's a lot more spots where the bass and drums are spotlighted as opposed to the guitar. And "Outta Love Again" is one of the songs where I think the drumming is real good.

GW The next song is "Somebody Get Me a Doctor."

VAN HALEN That was one written around the same time as "Runnin' with the Devil." It was an old favorite of ours and people who used to follow us around before we ever had a record out. Basically what we do in the studio is we sit with Ted and we pick out which songs we want to do. One out of the four of us might say, "Hey, let's do this one" and the other guys will go, "Nah, why don't we try this one?" So "Somebody Get Me a Doctor" didn't make the first record. It's about being high and feeling good and ODing and stuff like that.

The next one is "Women in Love" and that's a trippy one. If you follow the lyrics you can look at it two ways: It's like a guy who is going out with a chick and as opposed to the conventional way of losing a chick to a guy, he loses his chick 'cause his chick runs off with another chick. You know—women in love!

GW What is happening at the beginning of the song?

VAN HALEN There are harmonics in the intro and it sounds different. It kinda sounds like I used a harmonizer but I didn't; all I did was double it. It sounds real neat. I used a regular Strat on that; I put it together myself. I have a Telly pickup in the back, a Fat Strat and something else. And I just had a junk body lying around and I threw it together in like a day and I had a Danelectro neck that I put on it. I only used it for one part; a quiet little intro. Because that other guitar is too ballsy sounding to play quiet and clean. That's about it for that one.

GW You did a cover song on this album?

VAN HALEN "You're No Good," which doesn't sound at all like the original. I've never actually heard the original. Linda Ronstadt didn't write the song. [*The song was written by Clint Ballard, Jr.—Ed.*] It's a great song, I think. We used to do that song when we played Gazzarri's, only we did it like the original record; we didn't do it our own way. When we were in the studio to record it I couldn't even remember how it went. I just started noodling around and that's how it came about. We never even listened to the record. I just remembered the changes and because I didn't listen to the record, it didn't sound the same. I just kinda thought back about the basics of the song and that's how it ended up. At least this way we'll be able to pull it off live.

GW Being able to play a song live is a consideration in not doing a lot of overdubs?

VAN HALEN Sure. That's the main reason we don't do a lot of overdubs. Like if I do something that's the main part of the song as an overdub and I can't do it live, people are gonna miss it. They'll say, "Hey, it doesn't sound the same." So when we do overdubs, they're real subtle little things that just enhance the sound as opposed to being a real melodic main thing or something. We just depend on the rhythm section and guitar for solos and singing for melody.

GW Talk about "Bottoms Up!"

VAN HALEN It's a proven song because in the 10 months we toured, six months of it at least we played it every night for our encore song everywhere from Texas to Japan—they loved it. There's a good solo in that one too. Personally, I hate soloing to boogies; it's such a weird beat and it doesn't really fit my style that well. I like to noodle out of the rhythm as opposed to playing in the beat, so I was pretty happy with it.

Then there's "Light Up the Sky," and that's my favorite. I wrote that song right after our first record was recorded. I used to dick around and play it for the guys and it was like, "Oh, Eddie's got a new riff," and nobody really said anything. And then when we came back off tour, we played all our new riffs and songs and whatever for Ted and he really liked that one. I was totally surprised because it was a little more progressive; the changes are a little more bent than the commercial and simple stuff. So I was happy that he liked that.

GW What else is on the new album?

VAN HALEN "Beautiful Girls" is a happy one. [*plays the riff on the guitar*] The theme of that song is pretty much, "I got a drink in my hand, I got my toes in the sand/I'm feelin' good with a beautiful girl." It's a happy song to kind of balance it out. I hate some records; you listen to it and it's just happy-happy all the way through. There's a way to write a song where the music is up but it's still got a serious type of theme and we got a little bit of both on this record. Some songs that sound real happy, poppy, sing-along type of stuff and the other stuff is drinking a bottle of booze and fucking. That'll be a good one, I think—I like it on the tape. "D.O.A." is a good one too. Just being an outlaw and everybody is out to get you—dead or alive type of thing.

Then there's Mike's bass solo, which we need to call something. It's up to him. I named my solo "Eruption" because it kinda sounded like it. I don't know what Mike should call his bass solo. He might not win awards for being a great bass player but just the sound he gets out of it really makes a vibe; it sets a mood. When you hear it, you think of something as opposed to thinking, Oh, he's a good bass player. It sounds like animals or something—animals out late at night out to get you. It will probably be the intro into "You're No Good." Just like my solo was an intro to "You Really Got Me." If "You're No Good" is ever a single, I don't think it'll be on there. Just like "You Really Got Me" was a single and it didn't have the solo on it.

GW You must be really pleased with your playing on this album.

VAN HALEN Definitely. There's a lot of guitar tricks on it but some of them are more subtle than the last record—they're not as obvious. Like when you heard the harmonic thing, a lot of people won't even think it's a guitar but it is. I like doing stuff like that—just tricks where people trip when they find out it's a guitar. They go, "Whoa!" I read a review once of our first album and they didn't even think the finger thing that I did for "Eruption" was a guitar. They just bypassed it and said, "Oh, a synthesizer solo by Edward Van Halen." I just tripped out; if this guy took the time to find out what I was doing he'd know it was a guitar.

GW Have you thought about maybe adding keyboards to the sound of the band?

VAN HALEN When we recorded the first album, I had no idea what this next one would be like. To me it's a logical progression but it still sounds like Van Halen. There have been bands who put out one record and the next one sounds too different. Have you ever heard of a band called Stray Dog? Their first album is great and the second one sounds so different.

GW Are there any acoustics on the album?

VAN HALEN Yeah. There's one song that we still might do, an acoustic song called "Angel Eyes." It's a real neat song. Dave wrote the melody and chord changes. He plays acoustic somewhat; he used to do solo stuff before. That's where "Ice Cream Man" came from; he used to play that acoustic at the Ice House [*club in Pasadena*] all the time. We just said, "Hey, why don't you do that and we'll just come in halfway through?" And "Angel Eyes," I think the reason we might not put it on is because it's too much of a change. It's a total acoustic song and I think people might look at it like, "Oh, they had to stick one on there just for the hell of putting it on." So we probably won't because if we did put it on that ain't why we'd do it—it's just a good song. So maybe later on when we are doing different things, it'll fit better.

GW What you played for me sounded pretty ballsy.

VAN HALEN This album, to me, sounds heavier than the first—the overall sound is just so much fuller. The songs might not be based on riffs as much as the first, but in my mind I still consider it harder sounding. But smoother too...I don't know how to explain it.

GW More mature?

VAN HALEN Yeah. It's not as rough—it's got more tone and more confidence in the playing. It just feels more sure.

GW Do you sit in on the mixing sessions?

VAN HALEN Uh, no. It doesn't really take that much to mix it. Like what you heard sounds decent to me and it's not even mixed. Just put everything at the same level and there you go. See, that's why it's so simple...because there's not a bunch of shit. "Oh, pull this up" and stuff like that. It's just three instruments playing at the same levels, so what the hell? You don't have to juggle it around and pop this in here and there. Simple. I'm not saying that it's that simple to mix but it's not that hard. It's gonna be obvious if something's lost because if the guitar is lost all you hear is bass and drums.

GW When does the album come out?

VAN HALEN February 10th as far as I know; maybe even sooner because it's going so quick [Van Halen II *was actually released on March 23, 1979—Ed.*]. We recorded the 10 songs in four days of recording and the singing should go quick too because it's all rehearsed and ready to go.

GW You really are able to get a performance in just one or two takes?

VAN HALEN Oh, yeah! If you listen to this tape right here, "Dance the Night Away," you can hear him say, "Take two" right before it. We haven't cut that off yet because it's just a rough tape. We never do more than three or four takes of any song because you lose the vibe, you lose the feeling, you lose that pocket. That thing where everyone's really together. I find that I work best the first three hours. The first half-hour I'm kinda nervous and I've got to loosen up and drink a couple of beers and near the tail end of the first hour I'm cookin' along and for the next couple of hours too. But after that my mind's drained—my head's a vegetable after that. I can play but I can't be creative—I can't think, I can't write. It's rewarding writing a song but the studio is also real hard on your head.

GW Even the solos come out best on the first pass?

VAN HALEN Oh, sure. Usually they're better that way. But sometimes the song itself isn't as good. The first take is always just like a run-through and sometimes it is the take but usually that's when I solo best because I'm not thinking. After three, four times I start thinking, God, it ain't going so good. I've got to do it right. And you start thinking so much that you blow it.

GW You won't ever work on a solo at home before coming into the studio?

VAN HALEN No, I didn't do that at all this time. I did it last time on a couple things; I just sat down to think, Fuck, man, what kind of solo am I gonna do to this? I think it was "Ice Cream Man," that weird lick was kind of set. Yesterday I did like three overdubs and I surprised myself. I just stand in there and drink half a bottle of wine and it really felt good. The rest of the guys were all partying and I was the only who worked all day yesterday. But still everyone comes down drinkin' beers and smokin' a joint and yelling, "Heyyy, yeah, Ed, that sounds good!"

GW The stuff that I heard and the sound of your guitar was really amazing.

VAN HALEN Thank you. I was kind of surprised because it sounded better this time than the first album, I think. It sounds different.

GW It sounds so live. How are you able to baffle and separate the instruments and still get such a sort of live and organic quality?

VAN HALEN Mainly because everything is just stacked up and blazing away. When I did overdubs, I just used one cabinet as opposed to five or six blasting away. But usually I just face my cabinets away from Al's drum mikes, maybe with a little partition around the drums. With us it's not that important either to get that much separation. I mean it is to a point to keep it clean but when you have a lot of instruments and guitar bleeding on drum mikes and bass coming in through guitar mikes, it really garbles things up. But with us it just makes it sound more live.

"I smoke **too many cigarettes** and drink **too many beers.**"

GW Do you do any singing on the record?

VAN HALEN I do backup singing; I don't think I'll ever lead sing. I don't like singing live too much because I smoke too many cigarettes and drink too many beers. I jump around and I like to concentrate on playing more. I used to sing in the early days before we ever had Dave in the band; I used to lead sing. It was me, Al, and a different bass player [*Mark Stone*]. I used to sing all the Sabbath stuff and Grand Funk and Cream.

GW Do you live with the band in Pasadena?

VAN HALEN We did before we got signed; we all lived in one big house. But now me and Al both live at home with our parents. Dave lives with his dad and Mike lives with his parents. We all live close together but at the time all of our parents just had it up to here with rock and roll. So we all moved in together in this big house and everyone pitched in for rent. We had chicks living there too to cook for us and wash the clothes. It was kinda neat actually, but now our parents will have us once again.

GW Will you go back out on the road again after the album comes out?

VAN HALEN I'd sure like to do a local gig somewhere before we take off. New Year's Eve at the Whisky would have been great but Dave busted his foot and it's kind of a drag. I really enjoy playing; I don't know what else to do. I think the main reason why we didn't burn out on the road even though we've been out for so fucking long is that we really enjoy playing. The high point of the day would be when we walked onstage. It's not work. The work part is traveling and that at times wasn't so bad. But sometimes you have to take three planes to go in circles and you go nowhere. I remember once we had to get to Bay City, Michigan, and we were in Texas and instead of taking one flight up we had to go to Denver and then to Chicago. We were almost home in Denver and then we had to go all the way back to Michigan and we'd get up there and do an in-store, go by a couple of radio stations, and by that time I'm burned out. When we walked onstage, even if I was dead, I still get off playing.

GW How did Dave break his foot?

VAN HALEN Oh, yeah, let me tell you about that. The picture on the back of the cover is the shot where he broke his foot. It is a trippy picture when you see it. He's way up in the air with his feet out and with the mic and the funny thing is he's still holding onto the mic stand. He's wearing Capezio dance shoes which are no good if you're bouncing up and down on cement. He really wrecked up his foot. And then on the inside Dave is sitting there with a cane and a cast on his foot.

GW Have you made a lot of money so far?

VAN HALEN I don't know yet; we've got to meet with our accountants next week to see what we've made. It sounds funny, man, but I still feel like a kid; it still hasn't fazed me. Even if I made a lot of money, I don't know what the fuck to do with it. I went out and bought myself a $700 car. What the fuck? I still live at home. The first thing I'm going to do is get my dad to retire. Even just weekly checks out of our corporation we're making more than he is a week. So Al and I said, "Quit your job." He's been working seven days a week ever since we came to this country and we're gonna buy him a boat and retire him so he can go fishing.

[5]

"I don't really think I get better.
I just change."
—EDDIE VAN HALEN

THIRD POWER

Shortly before the March 1980 release of Van Halen's third record, *Women and Children First*, Eddie Van Halen sat with writer Steven Rosen to discuss the band's most varied album to date.

BY STEVEN ROSEN

Lost Interview #3

GUITAR WORLD What has the process been like for this third album?

EDDIE VAN HALEN It's hard for me to tell you. It seems like it's taken so long but it's all been the red tape stuff. We did all the music, the actual recording, in four days except for the acoustic song; we did that at the very end. And then the week after that we sang for four days.

GW There are a lot of new textures on the record, like electric piano.

VAN HALEN Yeah, I play piano on "And the Cradle Will Rock..." We were doing a bus tour last year and we said, "Well, what are we gonna do different on the next record?" So I said, "What the hell?" I'll go out and buy a little Wurlitzer and plink on it and that's how I came up with the music for that. That was first take by the way, except for the guitar overdubs, which I did later because I can't play piano and guitar at the same time. And no one else in the band can play guitar.

GW How will you pull that off live?

VAN HALEN Mike's gonna play it [*electric piano*]. My brother said, "Don't play piano. Don't be a Sammy Davis, Jr., a jack-of-all-trades and master of none. Just stick to guitar." So Mike is gonna play key bass like the Doors used to use, one of those Rhodes key bass things and a Wurlitzer piano. We all pretty much play keyboards but I did write the song and play it on the record.

Let me tell you about the piano song because that's a rather unusual sound for a piano. I blazed it through my little pedal board and my Marshalls and the noise that you hear in the beginning is just an MXR flanger and banging on the lower register of the piano. In doing that, I busted one of the keys on my piano. But for better or worse, it came out on the record.

GW What is the song about?

VAN HALEN It's about a kid you might say who is deprived of rock and roll but the cradle will rock—no matter what happens to him he's still gonna rock.

GW Like the first two records, there aren't many overdubs on this one?

VAN HALEN I overdubbed the solo on "And the Cradle Will Rock..." and the solo is overdubbed on "Everybody Wants Some!!" because it's melodic. I prefer to overdub set melodic solos. Like on the first album I would do the solo and overdub the rhythm track. If it was a melodic solo, I would play the solo on the basic track and then overdub a rhythm. But this time Ted [*Templeman, producer*] thought it would flow better if I just played rhythm all the way through. And the very end of "Fools" I overdubbed a basic guitar.

But that's it, so there's actually three overdubs on guitar. Oh, and on "Simple Rhyme" I overdubbed the 12-string.

GW Had you played much 12-string before this?

VAN HALEN No, it was a hassle and a half tuning the damn thing, though. I swear to God, man, we got this funky SIR Rickenbacker job with six-month old rusted strings on it and shit.

GW It almost sounds like an acoustic 12-string.

VAN HALEN I just played it real quiet. I played it direct and miked it so it sounds like an acoustic guitar, but it still has kind of an electric sound to it.

GW Tell me about some of the other songs.

VAN HALEN "And the Cradle Will Rock..." was brand new, "Everybody Wants Some!!" and "Romeo Delight" were brand new, and "Could This Be Magic?" was brand new and the intro and shit. "Loss of Control" we reworked so it wouldn't sound as punk. I wrote it at the same time I wrote "Ain't Talkin' 'Bout Love." "Whiskey" [*Take Your Whiskey Home*] was an old song and we decided to change that a bit with the acoustic intro. Everything else is new; there are only two songs on here that were worked out before we went into the studio. "Could This Be Magic?" is the acoustic song where we sound like a bunch of drunk fool sailors just getting into town. Actually the hook of the album title is in that: "Better save the women and children first." But it's not the title track.

GW What is the title of the album?

VAN HALEN *Women and Children First*, but we decided to call the song "Could This Be Magic?" so all the radio program directors wouldn't play that song first if we called it "Women and Children First."

GW There's some slide in "Could This Be Magic?"

VAN HALEN The first time I ever played slide. We were a little bit drunk and the guys go, "Doesn't sound right, Ed, why don't you try playing slide?" I'm going, "Uh oh, I've never played slide, guys." They're going, "Just fake it." I just played it regular guitar tuning; I didn't re-tune. A lot of people tune especially for slide; I don't even know how to tune it that way. I just played it normal.

GW There are a lot of these little intro bits that musically stand on their own and really have nothing to do with the songs that follow.

VAN HALEN Yeah. "Tora! Tora!" is the introduction to "Loss of Control," which is kind of appropriately titled. It sounds like a Spitfire taking off or something.

GW How did you do that intro?

VAN HALEN I did it with one of those Floyd Rose vibrato bar things.

GW When we were listening to the tape, you pointed out these little phrases that were actually wrong notes and stuff. But you left them in.

VAN HALEN Sometimes I do shit on a record, man, and it's just a freak little thing. I love mistakes because you can never re-do them exactly the same; you never can. They're just freak things. And a lot of times some good shit comes out.

"It was a hassle and a half tuning the 12-string."

GW "Fools" has a little mistake in it?

VAN HALEN Yeah, I don't even know how I did it; it was really a freak thing. It sounds weird; it sounds like I'm slipping. It's just one of those things where you say, "Wait a minute...what is that?" I wasn't sure whether I liked it or not but then since I couldn't exactly figure out how I did, I said, "Yeah, I like it."

GW No solo songs like "Eruption" or "Spanish Fly"?

VAN HALEN No, I did a small introduction to "Fools," which is a little guitar freakout for a couple seconds. That should fulfill the guitar freaks.

"**Nobody will play with us.**"

GW Your homemade Strat is still the main guitar?

VAN HALEN Yeah, it's the only one I used. Oh, wait, I used a 335 for the solo in "And the Cradle Will Rock..." For some reason when I play a 335, I can really blaze fast. It's just a different feel for a guitar.

GW What about live?

VAN HALEN Yeah. I just had Linn Ellsworth make me a Strat body; it's as thick as a Les Paul. Real fat, made out of mahogany and I'm in the process of painting it. It's real heavy but it gets a lot of tone. Using the Floyd Rose tremolo thing which I like and I don't like—it has its advantages and disadvantages—I have gotten used to using it live. So that's pretty much what I do use live. I have it on one guitar so far; it'll be on the new one. For some reason, the metal his tremolo is made out of is real brittle sounding. And I've tried everything to get a tone out of the damn thing and I couldn't. I had it on one guitar and I just couldn't get a sound out of it. So I had Linn Ellsworth make me a body twice as thick hoping that would make up for the brittleness of the metal.

GW You like the original Fender Strat tailpieces?

VAN HALEN I prefer the old tailpieces. For some reason they get a lot more tone than all this other garbage. Mighty Mite brass stuff. Brass?

I don't know, man, it just doesn't seem to work for me. I can't get a tone out of it. For some reason the old stuff is just the best. It manages to get the sound I like.

GW Is the whammy bar still a big part of what you do?

VAN HALEN I didn't freak out on the bar as much as I usually do. Just so it would sound a little different.

GW When you go back out on the road, will be doing a bunch of these new songs?

VAN HALEN Yeah, it's actually very difficult for us to figure out what to play now. We have three albums to choose from. It would seem easy to pick but actually it's harder to pick because we don't know which ones to do. Looking at it now with three albums' worth of material that we can play, I go, "God, I don't see how we pulled it off our first year with only eight songs to play." I'm sure we'll do more than half of this new album.

GW Which songs will you do?

VAN HALEN I know we'll do "And the Cradle Will Rock...," "Everybody Wants Some!!" "Romeo Delight," "Loss of Control" and "Simple Rhyme." And we're debating on whether we're gonna do "Could This Be Magic?" which is the acoustic song. I think we might do that instead of "Ice Cream Man" because it's nice to have an acoustic song in the set.

GW Do you pick the bands that open for you on tour?

VAN HALEN Actually the bands that we pick won't play with us. Nobody will play with us. It's hard. Come one, come all—we're not afraid of anybody. They're afraid. Last year every band that played with us got booted off somewhere along the line. Seriously it really freaked me out. Our first show last year was in Fresno and the Fabulous Poodles opened up and got booed off the stage. We don't want to pull a Zeppelin and just play two and a half hours by ourselves, because kids get tired of that.

GW Didn't you also have a problem with Rick Derringer?

VAN HALEN Yeah, I don't want to talk about that.

GW I had interviewed Rick a while ago and he was talking about guitar players and I said, "Who do you listen to?" and he said, "I listen to everybody. Eddie Van Halen is fantastic."

VAN HALEN He just acted like an asshole when I talked to him. For him to play like me or cop my style is fine. But to play my solo almost note-for-note and then go into our ending song, that's a little different. He's a nice guy and I had asked him, "Don't do exactly what we do," because that would be just like us playing it twice.

GW So are you happy with the album?

VAN HALEN Yeah, I love it. I think it's our best one yet because it's got more variety. It's not too guitar dominated; it's just got a little bit of everything on it. It's got acoustic, it's got piano, it's got the ball-bustin' rock. It's got it all.

GW Don't you think people listen to Van Halen specifically to hear your guitar playing and to see what new sounds you've created?

VAN HALEN I'm sure they listen to it for the overall thing. I don't think they listen to it just for my playing. But I think there's enough of my playing on there to satisfy them.

GW Have you ever thought about what people have come to expect from you as a guitar player? Is there pressure to keep constantly coming up with new stuff on the guitar?

VAN HALEN It seems like it would but it doesn't. 'Cause the way I've gotten to where I've gotten is just by doing what I do without worrying about, "Oh, I gotta do this. I gotta make sure I get better." I don't really think I get better. I just change. You can only get so fast, you can only twang so much. It's a matter of change more, I think, than getting better. I think it's changed from the first album to the second and from the second to the third. I don't want to call it maturing or anything. If you're exposed to different things you tend to play different now and then. And right now I'm playing a little different than I have in the last couple of years. It still sounds like me. I still think you'll be able to pick up on the sound and the style right away but I'm using a different combination of notes now and then. Playing different licks and different riffs and different little noises. There's noises on this record that people probably wouldn't even know what it is. Sure, there are certain licks that I do consciously and the best ones usually come out when I'm not thinking.

GW Do you hear other people playing like Eddie Van Halen?

VAN HALEN I'm not trying to sound egotistical but they try to. And I actually think it's better that they try to because it comes off as a little different. Whereas if they play exactly like me it's gonna sound like me. Just like when I grew up playing, I tried playing exactly like some people but I just couldn't. I think that's how my style developed. Out of the mere fact that I couldn't play like someone else. I had to do something, I had to come up with something myself.

GW Is there any new music that you like?

VAN HALEN I love Allan Holdsworth. I'm into the last album he did with Bruford. It still amazes me every time I hear it. That fucker is good. U.K. opened for us once in Reno and I couldn't believe it. I shit my pants. They're going, "U.K. is opening for you." I said, "Okay, groovy." I never heard of U.K. And then all of a sudden I looked at Al and said, "Isn't that Bill Bruford?" These guys were fucking playing but the people weren't very receptive to them at all. Goddamn that dude is really a strange player. It sounds like he doesn't pick a lot, that's why it sounds so smooth. You can never hear the attack of his pick. I'd love to hear him play with [*Tim*] Bogert. If I ever played bass, that's how I'd want to play. Put it that way. That's what I don't understand—that he's not that respected or that famous for being that good. It's almost like Holdsworth. He's so fucking good but he doesn't get the credit.

GW What about people like Ted Nugent and Ace Frehley?

VAN HALEN Ted is a nice guy but I don't really like the way he plays too much. He looks at it like Gene Simmons. Gene is a real nice guy; he always writes us. He wanted me and Al to play on his solo album but we couldn't because we were on tour. A couple songs on the record we played on the demo tape and they sounded much better. They sounded real good; I liked 'em. "Tunnel of Love," but it's done different; it's half-beat on this one but it was more rock when me and Al played it. And the other one was "Christine Sixteen." Remember the solo in that? I wrote the solo for that and it sounded so good when we played with him because I double-tracked it. It was a double solo, a double lead. It sounded so good and then all of a sudden their record comes out [Love Gun] and they played the same solo but it sounded like he used some kind of octave box. It didn't sound the same. "That guy, he fucked up my solo." It sounded good; it was a good melodic little thing that really fit in.

I was surprised with Ace Frehley's solo album. I liked it. It's just more "up." At least he stepped out a little bit. I mean, he's not that great of a guitarist either. The way he plays sounds so uncoordinated. I don't want to sit here and cut all these people down. I always still look at myself like a kid looking at these guys like they're big. I don't know, I just don't look at myself equal to them. So I find myself cutting them down, but I don't really mean to. Sometimes these guys just play with a weird kind of vibrato and they always seem to miss the note. They go everywhere around it [*picks up a guitar and mimics a very bad guitar player with a lifeless finger vibrato*].

GW Ted Templeman and Donn Landee obviously worked on this one.

VAN HALEN Oh, yeah, did a great job, I think. Excellent job.

GW They must be used to the Van Halen system of madness by now.

VAN HALEN Yeah, I think it's a breath of fresh air for them. Everything else they do is very middle of the road to mellow. We are the only rock thing that they produce. Even out of rock bands, I think we lean to the extreme.

[6]

"We do whatever we want
to do and that's it."
—EDDIE VAN HALEN

SO THIS IS LOVE

As Van Halen's 1982 album *Diver Down* raced up the charts, Eddie Van Halen looked back with great fondness on that album's monumental predecessor, 1981's *Fair Warning*.

BY STEVEN ROSEN

I N MANY WAYS, *Fair Warning* was the least understood of all the Van Halen albums. Today, veiled rumblings still echo about the record's latent darkness, the lack of a big single and the unorthodox sound and style of many of its tracks. Yet for those willing to see past all of that and wade into the rivers of guitars so intelligently orchestrated, what awaited them was a baffling array of six-string motifs, intersecting walls of rhythm, and solos gloriously and passionately executed. Everyone knows about the invention and imagination on *Van Halen* and the keyboards and charisma of *1984*. But sandwiched between the two is an oft-times overlooked miracle of electric guitar, a savage and compelling vision from the most important instrumentalist to emerge in the last two and a half decades.

This conversation took place in 1982 immediately following the release of *Diver Down*. Obviously Edward addressed the newest album but felt that in order to put it more in perspective, it was necessary to look back at the one that came before. Hunkered down in the living room of his Coldwater Canyon home, frosty beers and mixed drinks flowing nicely, he revisited *Fair Warning* to reveal the secrets and sacrifices surrounding that record's genesis. Clutching an unplugged electric guitar for ballast, Van Halen punctuated his responses by playing the various riffs being discussed. Even acoustically, these bits and pieces sounded as big as heaven crashing.

GUITAR WORLD *Fair Warning* was different than the earlier albums. On the first three records you tended to minimize overdubs while on this one you seemed to focus on multiple guitar parts.

EDDIE VAN HALEN Oh, yeah, I think the most ever. I did a lot of overdubbing and it came out real good, I think. It was a very different approach from my standpoint, and I'm very happy with it—and I love the solos that I did. I'm not in the slightest way unhappy with any solo I did on that record; I like 'em all.

GW Was this a technique you specifically wanted to try? Or did the songs demand this sort of elaborate treatment?

VAN HALEN I gotta say that, okay, *Fair Warning*, out of our five albums, was done, most of it, the complete opposite of *Diver Down*. Most of it was done in the studio.

GW The songs were worked up in the studio?

VAN HALEN Yes; I had basic ideas. We came off tour and everyone goes, "Whadd'ya got, Eddie?" and I showed them basic ideas and we went from there. Instead of working them up before we went in the studio, we worked them out *in* the studio. And I think I'm doing some of my best solos on that record.

I don't know if this sounds egoed out but I kind of amaze myself sometimes when I look back at the tunes and the music that I've written. I think it's good; I'm going, "Goddamn." I mean, on *Fair Warning*, everything on it I came up within two weeks. I also weighed 125 pounds; I lost a lot of weight and a lot of sleep because I knew it had to be done.

I mean, like, "Sinner's Swing!" was spontaneous; that was a first take. It sounds like falling down the stairs. I like the solo in "Push Comes to Shove" too—actually, I like every solo that I did on that record. including "Unchained" and the one on "Hear About It Later" with those little countermelodies.

Fair Warning is the most expensive album we've done so far, though. It took longer and you can blame that on me—it's my fault, but I just wanted to approach it different. I wanted to do more over-dubbing so it took time. But I like it all; it fits.

GW The way you start the solo in "Push Comes to Shove" with those simple hammers and that minor feel just sends shivers up your spine.

VAN HALEN Because it was a break and everything stopped.

GW It just cries out with this thematic melody. In fact it sounds like it's the opening notes of a movie score.

VAN HALEN That's the only solo ever in my life except for "Secrets" [*Diver Down*] and "Push Comes to Shove" that I semi worked out. I worked out the beginning of "Secrets" and especially the last part; I planned it. And I might have done a couple of takes of it and one was better than the other but they were all basically pretty much the same. And "Push Comes to Shove" and "Secrets" are the only two songs ever on any album that I planned.

GW "Push Comes to Shove" was a real different type of track for the band. Sort of a combination of the Stones, R&B, funk and reggae.

VAN HALEN Oh, definitely; I think "Secrets" is, too.

GW Do you think that "Push Comes to Shove" was a sort of stepping-stone to creating "Secrets"? Not that either song vaguely resembles the other.

VAN HALEN Yeah, I know what you mean. What I think about the band is that you cannot label us. You cannot call us heavy metal; you cannot call us progressive; you cannot call us mellow; you cannot call us whatever you want to call us. We do whatever we want to do and that's it. Take it or leave it. If you don't like it, you don't like it; if you do, you do. But we do what we want to do. Period.

GW Do you have any feelings about David Lee Roth's vocals on the album?

VAN HALEN The truth is, I don't think he sang as good as I played. He took off for two weeks and again it was, "What do you got, Eddie?" and I had pretty much basic ideas for everything that is on the record. I worked my ass off on that one. But I love it; it's my life. At least Dave pulls his weight. Mike [*Anthony, bass*] doesn't. He doesn't do anything; he has no input whatsoever. Period. But he has remodeled his whole house and bought himself a Turbo Carrera off the money he's made off of us. Whatever.

GW How exactly do you and Dave work on a track? Do you present him with a piece of music and suggest melodies and places in the song where you hear a verse or chorus?

VAN HALEN Here's what happens: I come up with the music. Like 99.9 percent I have every part then Alex usually hears everything I come up with before anyone else. And then sometimes Ted [*Templeman, producer*]. So the music comes first. Then melody is applied and then lyrics.

GW But where does that melody come from?

VAN HALEN Depends. Dave writes 99.9 percent of the lyrics. A lot of times we don't like a word here and there and we'll change it. I'd say melody comes from Dave a lot, comes from Al [*Alex Van Halen, drums*] a lot, and I am more involved in the music than anything else.

GW When you wrote these tracks, you must have heard melodies running through them. In fact, what makes the guitars on this album so compelling is that many of the overdubs you play sound like they may have been vocal lines.

VAN HALEN Yeah, but then again, we're coming to a point that I can't talk about which is Dave's range.

GW On the musical side, when you listen to some of the tracks, there are times when the only instrument you can hear coming out one side of the speaker is a rhythm guitar or drums. The bass is almost non-existent.

VAN HALEN Right—it's guitar and nothing on the other side. Why don't I play you some of the stuff that I did at home? And you can hear right there, it's just a bass straight into my goddamn 4-track Teac and that sounds better than what Mike does.

GW The guitars on the album are so beautifully composed and structured that it must make it infinitely more difficult to perform them without the support of the bass.

VAN HALEN It doesn't make it harder to play because I'll tell you the honest-to-God fucking truth—that since day one, I never liked Mike's sound and I could never hear him. I can never hear him play when we play. Period. All I have live in my monitors is Al, a little bit of Dave's vocals, a little bit of mine, a little bit of Mike's, and all I hear is myself and my brother. In the studio, it's the same.

GW Which brings us to another remarkable aspect of the album and that is the rhythm playing. Your sense of rhythm is so highly developed—is that how you're able to pull off these parts without hearing a bass track?

VAN HALEN I don't know. I am absolutely a rhythmic player. I work more off of rhythm than I do...I'm not saying that I'm not melodic at all. I can be melodic if I want to be. But most of my spontaneous stuff is not melodic; it does have a certain edge to it where it goes high, low, in-between, slow, fast and whatever. But that's why I like "Push Comes to Shove," which I think is melodic, and "Secrets" is melodic and maybe even the solo on "Dancing in the Streets" or whatever.

The other night I went over to Frank Zappa's house and played him *Fair Warning* all the way through and I was listening and I was amazed. I'm going, "I did that?" Frank tripped. He was going, "I thought you guys were just another fuckin' AC/DC!" When I talked to him on the phone [*Edward spent a fair amount of time over at Zappa's house while working on music with son Dweezil—Ed.*], the first thing he said to me was, "Thank you very much for reinventing the electric guitar."

GW Getting back to the album, what about "Hear About It Later"? There are layers of guitars on that track.

VAN HALEN Yeah. That was a heavy problem during mixing; Ted and Donn [*Landee, engineer*] were freaking out because I did so much guitar stuff that they didn't know what to use when and where. And Dave did so much screaming and yelling over some parts of it that they didn't know what to use of whatever.

GW The intro is a perfect example of those mountains of guitars. It segues from those dark legato chords at the very beginning into that hellish explosion of strings.

VAN HALEN In the beginning it's a clean Strat; the whole basic track was played with a clean Strat with a flanger on it and my regular red and white main guitar that I use for all the other stuff. And at the very end I didn't know what to do because Dave was yelling and screaming over it. So what they ended up doing was taking the background vocals out and the rhythm guitar too, I think. It was just bass and drums and the rhythm track slowly faded in and the background vocals and that last bit. I did a lot of overdubbing on it and I had a great time; it was fun.

GW "Sunday Afternoon in the Park" was the next step up keyboard-wise from "And the Cradle Will Rock..."

VAN HALEN Yeah. I do a lot of weird things, put it that way. I pulled out my slide on "Dirty Movies" and I hardly ever use it.

GW You played me basic four-track recordings of the early genesis of some of these songs and your sound was already there. What is it exactly that Donn does to shape the track?

VAN HALEN He believes in me. He likes what I like. Donn is the interpreter. All Ted does is say, "Cut out a few bars here and there" and that's it.

GW Which is important.

VAN HALEN Very important. But when you read reviews and stuff and they're saying, "Templeman is their sound." Ted had nothing to do with mixing this record. It was Donn who has mixed every record. And *Fair Warning* and *Diver Down*, I was in on.

GW How does *Fair Warning* match up with *Diver Down*?

VAN HALEN *Fair Warning* compared to *Diver Down* didn't seem like it fit together.

GW No continuity?

VAN HALEN No. I listened to *Fair Warning* again the other night and I was blown away. I'm going, "Wow, it's a lot better than I fucking thought it was." But *Diver Down* seemed to have a more band attitude;

more Ted and Donn and the group as opposed to *Fair Warning. Fair Warning* was more separated; what's the word I'm looking for? It wasn't as together as a band, I guess.

GW You obviously feel very strongly about your work on the album. What was the response from fans and everyone else?

VAN HALEN What kind of baffles me is everyone's opinion is that it's kind of out there; that it's weird or different. Hard to relate to compared to anything else we've done. I don't see that. To me, it was more like the first album than *Van Halen II* or *Women and Children First*. It was more straightforward rock. Like "Unchained," c'mon, that's a blazer. The only different things were "Sunday Afternoon in the Park" and "Push Comes to Shove." Everything else was like "I'm the One," a quick boogie. "Hear About It Later" was kinda like the same beat or styled song as "Ain't Talkin' 'Bout Love." I think if anything *Women and Children First* was the one that I thought would strike people as stepping out because of "Could This Be Magic" and "In a Simple Rhyme" and things like that. That's what I really don't understand, because everybody says, "Wow, it's a kinda weird album." And I'm goin', "What the fuck? Are you looking at the album cover or are you listening to it?" I think maybe that had a little subconscious influence on people's minds just because the album cover was so bizarre. But the music, I think, was very straightforward.

"I do a lot of weird things."

[7]

"Lots of people think a song without singing is not a song. Tell that to Beethoven and he'll kick your ass."

—EDDIE VAN HALEN

THE LIFE AND TIMES OF VAN HALEN

As "Jump" hit *Billboard*'s Number One slot in 1984, *Guitar World* presented one of the first interviews from 5150, Edward's new home studio.

BY STEVEN ROSEN

DWARD VAN HALEN, born in Nijmegen, the Netherlands, on January 26, 1957, has been disseminating what he calls "the brown sound" now for over six years, or since the Pasadena quartet released its self-titled debut album. *Van Halen* sold over two million copies, with every subsequent release—*Van Halen II, Women and Children First, Fair Warning, Diver Down* and *1984*—selling well in excess of one million units. *1984* finished sixth on *Billboard*'s Top Albums of 1984; the "Jump" single ranked sixth as well, after occupying the coveted Number One position for a time.

   1984 is the first album recorded at Edward's 16-track home studio, 5150 (a name derived from an L.A. police code for the criminally insane). The cohesive batch of songs on the album re-establishes the balance and atmosphere which were notably absent from the group's *Diver Down* effort. Edward also establishes himself as a formidable synthesist on such tracks as the title song, "I'll Wait" and, of course, "Jump."

Coming off yet another world tour, Edward recently set aside several days to discuss *1984*, and the music he made prior to this breakthrough sixth album. Most of the conversations took place at 5150, amidst scattered guitars, reels of two-inch tape and empty beer cans. Rarely was the studio phone silent for more than an hour during our time together; it was during the unlikely lapses that much of the following interview took place.

Edward's schedule, even by a musician's standards, is a severe one. He ordinarily works from early evening to well past noon, experimenting with new guitars, programming rhythms on his LinnDrum and working on bits and pieces of music stashed on hundreds of scattered cassettes. "Noodling," he calls it.

Van Halen is wary of interviews—and interviewers—but quite adept at fielding questions. He is deliberate with his responses, and refreshingly forthright. As a result, what follows is a genuinely intimate look at the guitarist who, more than anyone since the golden days of the late Sixties, has redefined the limits of the electric six-string.

Eddie Van Halen's character hasn't changed. He is truly taken aback by compliments. Despite his enormous success, he is the same self-effacing man he was years ago, when the Van Halen group first signed with Warner Bros.

Here, then, is Edward Van Halen—father of the "brown sound."

GUITAR WORLD 1984 was a productive year for Van Halen.

EDWARD VAN HALEN The best year we've had. We started to see not just success, but also the satisfaction of knowing what we can accomplish. It was a strong year in every aspect.

GW Do you think it's the best music you've made?

VAN HALEN That's hard to say. I like everything we've done.

GW Did you think the *1984* album would be so well-received?

VAN HALEN I figured that it was good and would get noticed. But how can anyone say, "This is going to go Platinum"?

GW Are you the final arbiter of what eventually makes it on record?

VAN HALEN I'm not the only one involved. If the rest of the guys don't like something, I'm outvoted. But with regard to my happiness about something we've recorded, what I think of it is more important. If I like it and other people don't, of course my reaction might be, "Why don't they like it?" But I don't write to please other people. It's nice, but you have to please yourself first.

GW You've written songs that never made their way to vinyl.

VAN HALEN That's because Ted [*Templeman, Van Halen producer*] or somebody in the band voted against it, and decided it wasn't right for that point in time. "House of Pain" [1984] was written before we were signed. A lot of things I write aren't accepted with open arms, whether it's because of the instrumentation or that they just don't like the music.

GW What if you feel very strongly about a particular song?

VAN HALEN "I'll Wait" [1984] was one. Donn [*Landee, Edward's engineer*] and I both felt very strongly about it. Nobody else did, so we put it down ourselves. Then they heard it and said [*in dumb-struck tone*], "Uh, what's that?" I'm not going to sit there and cry if they don't like it, but sometimes something gets lost in the translation of an idea.

GW Does that happen very often?

VAN HALEN Obviously, it happens a lot. But the thing is, when you put it down on tape and they still don't like it, then there isn't a whole lot of room for miscommunication.

GW Do you think the difference in musical tastes between you and David Lee Roth has made Van Halen what it is?

VAN HALEN I'm sure that has had something to do with it, but it's not necessarily just Dave. It's Al and Ted and Donn and me all having different musical tastes. But it's not even musical tastes. Music is music, and if something is good and you like it, it's good. I like some jazz, I like some punk. Dave and Al listen to just about everything.

GW Do you bounce ideas off [*bassist*] Mike Anthony?

VAN HALEN I show my ideas to him along with everyone else. He generally goes along with the majority and usually doesn't have any strong preferences.

GW How close is the final version of a song to the original demo?

VAN HALEN Generally, there isn't much rewriting. Parts might be rearranged or chopped here and there.

GW Does Ted help with these arrangements?

VAN HALEN [*pauses*] Yes and no. He has a talent that, in a way, is unbeatable. But sometimes he doesn't allow other ideas to develop before he puts his this-is-the-way-to-go thing to it. And that's not putting him down at all. You can't expect any two people to think and feel identically about an idea. But that's how ideas get totally twisted and distorted from the original seed: people get involved in how they think it should sound. And I'm sure I'm as guilty of this as Ted and Al and Dave and everyone put together.

GW Where would you be if you had never gotten involved with Ted Templeman?

VAN HALEN I think we'd be where we are. But Ted tends to look for singles, or songs that could be a single for radio play; that's his way of thinking. We think differently. Period. I think we definitely complement him and vice-versa. Both parties would be different without the other. It's hard to say whether it would be better or worse. I think the reason we sound different is that the individuals in the band have their own styles.

GW Van Halen seems to be the yardstick by which every other rock band is measured. Do you think that's because you write great songs?

VAN HALEN What's a great song? Lots of people think a song without singing is not a song. Tell that to Beethoven and he'll kick your ass.

GW Would you like to have been Beethoven?

VAN HALEN I wouldn't want to have died at the age he did [57]. Anyone who wouldn't want to be as respected as he is would be a fool. I'm happy being who I am—I wouldn't want to be anybody else.

GW How would you say your songwriting has grown?

VAN HALEN It just changes. I guess, if I look back, I am better because I've been doing it longer. Or maybe it's easier. I'm more comfortable, more at ease constructing a song. But coming up with the ideas is just as difficult. That's why I say I don't know if I've grown.

GW But you probably have a better understanding of when the structure is right.

VAN HALEN Probably, yeah, but that's like saying, "Yes, I've been conditioned."

GW No, it's just that you're learning the craft.

VAN HALEN Yeah, but who's to say what's right? It's all within yourself—and, I guess, within myself I've gotten a better handle on what I feel is right.

GW When did you first start writing?

VAN HALEN I've probably been coming up with riffs ever since I picked up an instrument. It was probably around the time I played high school dances. Just to back up a bit, a main element you're leaving out in my own songwriting is Donn Landee. Donn and I work together at structuring things—I bounce everything off of him before anyone hears it.

GW So had Donn not been part of the picture from the beginning, Van Halen's sound might have been different?

VAN HALEN Definitely. And it would be harder.

GW Donn understands you pretty well.

VAN HALEN You said what I was trying to say. We understand each other well. To the point where the way he makes things sound is basically the way I hear things in my head. This is very unusual.

GW So what the public hears on the tape is the guitar sound you heard in your head?

VAN HALEN Within each given song. I can't say every record was exact. But I'm happy with everything on the last album [1984], and Donn and I worked very much as one on that. We're proud of it because it's something we felt was an accurate representation of what we were capable of. That goes for the band as a whole, too. But it was Donn's and my baby.

GW You haven't really written lyrics to any extent.

VAN HALEN It's not something I'm good at, or something I've spent any time with. A lot of times the way people write lyrics is so personal that nobody knows what the hell the words mean. Dave is that way. I don't even know the lyrics to our own songs, and it's no joke. Because a lot of the stuff is Dave's interpretation of life at that given moment. And even if he experienced it, it doesn't click concerning my life or the state of the nation. [*laughs*]

GW When you write the music, you must have some idea of what the song should say, lyrically.

VAN HALEN I never suggest to Dave what to write the lyrics about. Once he writes lyrics, Ted and Al and I suggest going this way or that way with it. I guess that's why sometimes I don't lean toward his lyrics, because something about them takes away from the mood the music creates, even covers that mood. It might take it to a better place—and sometimes not. Sometimes it takes away from the original feel of what is happening. And I can't exactly say, "Hey, it was sexy before and it isn't now." It's a feeling. Like, how do you explain [*sings opening notes of Beethoven's Fifth Symphony*]? What words would you say to that? When something sounds a certain way, I can't easily picture lyrics with it. Because it's pretty self-explanatory.

GW Like the opening to "1984"?

VAN HALEN Yeah; I couldn't hear any singing over that.

GW Is a lot of the music you listen to instrumental?

VAN HALEN Yeah, but I haven't listened to any of that stuff for at least a year. I don't even have a turntable or a cassette machine in the house.

GW Do you draw any inspiration from modern music?

VAN HALEN Let me put it this way: A lot of contemporary music wouldn't amount to much without lyrics. But I've seen a lot of lyrics and vocals ruin good music, in the same way opera singing over good classical music can do a heavy duty waste number on it. And who in the hell understands what they're saying in opera music? And how does someone in Japan, even though they may learn English in school, know what a person is saying? It's more the feeling. I'm not against vocals or lyrics; it's just a lot of times they rub me wrong.

GW Do you suggest vocal melodies?

VAN HALEN I try and help, yeah. Lines here and there. I never say, "Here's the music. Here's the melody. Fit words to these notes." Because that would be really ridiculous to say. Dave has done some stuff with the music that has been handed to him that has blown me away. Because some of the stuff I come up with is pretty twisted. Seriously. Twisted to the point where if he can squeeze a word or two in there or anywhere, he's got my vote. [*laughs*]

GW What are your feelings about Dave's solo album?

VAN HALEN I think it's something he always wanted to do. I think it's great he's actually doing it. Put it this way—it's something I've always wanted to do, and haven't done. I guess, in a funny way, it explains Dave as a vocalist and lyricist. He did four cover tunes—"California Girls," "Easy Street," "Just a Gigolo" and one other one—yet managed to project his personality through them. I expect it to be accepted by people in the same way everything we've done has been. I've heard it all and it sounds real good. Edgar Winter played a lot of stuff on it, and one of the Beach Boys actually sang on "California Girls." Ted produced it. It's Dave.

GW Did Dave want any of your input?

VAN HALEN No. It's something he wanted to do alone. He actually started doing it when Donn and I were doing the film soundtrack for *The Wild Life*. It's not that he didn't want it, but what's a solo project if you're going to have your band playing on it?

GW Do you think Dave wanted to have some original songs?

VAN HALEN Yeah, I guess. You'd have to ask him that, to tell you the truth. I think these were tunes that Dave feels a part of and always liked and wanted to re-do. I don't think he's out to prove anything. I know it will be good for him personally and his own self-satisfaction when it takes off the way I expect and hope it will. I seriously want the best for it, in the same way he'd want the best for me or Al or Mike if we did anything outside the band.

GW What are your solo plans?

VAN HALEN I don't have any plans.

GW Certainly there must be a record in you that wants to come out.

VAN HALEN I'd say there are a few. I haven't thought about it enough or talked to Donn about it enough. I guess in a way I look at it as something Donn and I could do whenever. It's not like something we feel we have to do in order to show anything, or for any other purpose. If the band decided to take a year off, then I could do it. But I don't want the band to take a year off because I'm doing it.

GW Speaking of vocals, weren't you the band's singer before Dave joined?

VAN HALEN Oh, yeah.

GW Is that when you were known as the Broken Combs?

VAN HALEN Broken Combs was the very first. Alex played saxophone and I played piano. This was in fourth or fifth grade. We actually had some original tunes, too. One called "Rumpus" and one called "Boogie Booger."

GW So you've been playing with Alex since day one?

VAN HALEN He's the only one I've ever played with, really.

GW Was there any competition between the two of you?

VAN HALEN No. What I couldn't do he made up for, and what he couldn't do I made up for. That's how he started playing drums. I used to play drums and he'd play 'em better, so I said, "Go ahead, you play 'em if you can do it better." I wasn't going to waste my time proving to my own brother that I could do it better.

GW Did you play violin?

VAN HALEN Yeah, for about three years. Al did, too. That was at the end of elementary school and the beginning of junior high. It was school-based stuff. Al actually made All City Orchestra on violin. I never did.

GW Did you find it difficult?

VAN HALEN I didn't like playing the songs they made me play, so I just started messing around with it and lost interest.

GW So from the outset, you never followed the rules.

VAN HALEN It seems that I didn't. But it wasn't intentional. I remember sitting there, pluckin' on the violin and playing along with the *Peter Gunn* series on TV.

GW Did your father want you to play violin or piano, as opposed to guitar?

VAN HALEN It's hard to say exactly what he wanted us to be; he wanted us just to be successful in life. Deep down he wanted it to be music. He wanted it to be piano, only to the extent that piano is the springboard to ear training—you can orchestrate your fingertips. Each finger is a different instrument. I've learned a lot from piano, and I play it more now than I have because I can play it the way I want to. No one is looking over my shoulder and saying, "No, that's wrong."

GW You had actual piano training?

VAN HALEN Yeah, from age six to 12. I was good. I actually won three first-prize trophies at Long Beach City College for my category in an annual contest. You sit there and practice one tune for the whole year, and they put you in a category and judge you. I think I won first place twice and second place the last time, which kind of showed I was losing interest. [*laughs*]

GW Did the feeling you had when you won first place mean anything to you?

VAN HALEN It didn't motivate me. After I played in the first contest, I sat in the bleachers while they held this beauty pageant countdown; I won and didn't even hear the guy say my name. So I just sat there and they passed by my category because they couldn't find me.

And finally, after the recap, they said, "Is Edward Van Halen here?" and I said, "What?" I guess the only thing it really did to me was make me more nervous for the next time. I didn't expect to win or lose. It wasn't like, "Wow, I won. I'm good!" It wasn't a motivation of any kind. I don't see why I won, to tell you the truth.

GW Did the piano training transfer itself to the guitar?

VAN HALEN Oh, definitely, but in a very subliminal way. Because I never learned how to read, really. I used to fool the teacher. I did it all by ear.

GW It wasn't important to you, to learn how to read?

VAN HALEN I guess the reason it didn't get me off in any way was that all it's good for is to learn how to play songs that have been written. And I told you the reason I didn't like violin was that I didn't like the songs we were supposed to play. I guess I was just a snot-nosed kid, and I didn't want to waste the time doing it. I'm sure I could have benefited from it, somehow. I can read, I know what the notes are, but I can't sight-read like Al can. He can open up anything and start playing. I never got close to that. I had to sit there and figure out the left-hand chord and I couldn't handle all those notes.

GW Was there much music in your house?

VAN HALEN Yeah, by my dad. In Holland I went with him when he used to play, but I was so young I don't remember. It wasn't the classical stuff then; he did that before he met my mother.

GW Your dad supported himself as a musician?

VAN HALEN Oh, yeah. As a matter of fact it was the only thing that pulled him through out here when we showed up in this country. We had $25 and a piano.

GW Did your dad make records?

VAN HALEN Yeah. I don't know exactly in what orchestra, but it wasn't "Blah blah blah featuring Jan Van Halen." It was a Philharmonic-type thing, and I have pictures of him standing up and soloing. He's probably on more records than I know.

GW Was your mom musical?

VAN HALEN Not professionally, but around the holidays my mom and dad jam. My mother has this huge organ with a rhythm box in it, and my dad whips out a sax and they play oldies.

GW Did your dad push you in that direction?

VAN HALEN No, he never discouraged us, but he didn't encourage us, either. I wanted to start playing saxophone, and I kind of felt he didn't want to spend the time. He struck me as being as impatient as I am when it comes to teaching someone something that is very difficult to teach. I don't mean the actual instrument, I mean the feeling behind it. My dad is into that so much that he doesn't even look at sax as an instrument of technical skills—it's secondary to the emotion involved.

GW How old were you when you got your first guitar?

VAN HALEN About 12 or 13. It was a flamenco Spanish guitar, but I didn't really consider it *my* guitar. It was Alex's, and he took classical guitar lessons while I banged away on the drums. I got left with his guitar when he started playing the drums, and decided to get an electric. It was a four-pickup $110 Teisco Del Ray from Sears. I liked it because it had the most pickups. It was fun.

GW Did you feel anything special when you picked up the electric for the first time?

VAN HALEN No, no message from God or anything. I thought it was neat. Some things were easy, some things were hard. I didn't even think about whether it was easy or hard; it was something I wanted to do, to have fun and feel good about doing it. Whether it took me a week to learn half a song or one day to learn five songs, I never thought of it that way.

GW Did you get an amplifier, too?

VAN HALEN I had an amp that was homemade by a friend of my dad's. The plug needed an adapter because it was a phono-plug. I got this weird adapter at Radio Shack and plugged my normal guitar cord into it, and turned the thing all the way up. It made a lot of noise and I started playing it while it was making all that noise. I remember Al walking in and going, "That sounds neat, man, what is that?" It was right around the time of that song, "Blues Theme" [*an instrumental by the Arrows*]. Al said, "Play that," and it sounded identical. It was crappin' out, distorted, nasty, so I guess that was my first exposure to that grungy noise.

GW When did you become aware of guitarists like Page, Beck and Clapton?

VAN HALEN I remember hearing Jimmy Page when a friend brought over the first Led Zeppelin album. And I tripped on it. I might have actually heard that before I heard Cream. My listening history is disjointed to me. I think I might have gotten into Cream, and then dug back to find the Bluesbreakers. I got into blues for a while and then went back to Cream. It wasn't that I was into blues and followed Clapton. I just knew I really dug him and then dug back and really got into a blues kick for six or eight months, or a year. Just jamming with guys, not really playing any songs, but jamming for hours on end, playing the same progression. Falling down the stairs and landing on your feet.

GW Your technique and style were developing here?

VAN HALEN Yeah, but it was just fun to do. I didn't think, If I do this for a year, I'll know this side of it. It was just a very natural thing; I wasn't doing anything for any purpose.

GW Did you say to yourself at this point, "I want to be a musician"?

VAN HALEN I have to think about when that was. I was still in junior high, so I wasn't the rebellious one—yet. Actually, I wasn't that rebellious anyway. I just managed to get myself into trouble without having to be rebellious. I never could get over how my friends could get away with murder and I was the only one to ever get caught at doing nothing.

GW What about the story of the time you were caught looking at the exam answers?

VAN HALEN Oh, yeah. Actually, I think Al was the one who told me about this, and I tried it and got caught. This English teacher, who was the only teacher I can remember who smoked, would leave the class during a test period and go off to the teacher's lounge and have a cigarette and my friends would go up to her desk and change grades. And I said, "Hell, I might as well do it, too." And right when I'm doing it the teacher walks in. Got nailed.

> "I managed to get myself into trouble without having to be rebellious."

GW Did bands like Mammoth come together while you where in high school?

VAN HALEN Yeah, ninth, tenth grade. Genesis was another band during that time. Then there was the Trojan Rubber Company. We also used to be called the Space Brothers. When we began playing high school dances and parties we had a hell of a reputation. This is funny because Al, Donn and I were just talking about this the other day—how it seems that only since Dave has been in the band did we get this rowdy and crazy brown cloud hanging over us. But we had it way before Dave was even in the band. Schools wouldn't hire us, nobody wanted anything to do with us, so we had to change the name of the band to the Space Brothers, just so we could play these gigs at a Catholic school.

GW What kinds of songs did you play?

VAN HALEN You name it: Grand Funk, Black Sabbath, Deep Purple, Cream...

GW Was Gazzarri's [*a local Hollywood club*] your first semi-professional gig?

VAN HALEN It was a breakthrough, yes. You know I got kicked out of clubs because I played too psychedelic.

GW You even had problems getting *into* Gazzarri's.

VAN HALEN Oh, yeah! We had to audition there at least three or four times. A guy would come running up in the middle of a song because I was too loud. But I didn't play that loud deliberately; the amp only sounded like an amp if it was all the way up. So I did everything—from keeping the plastic cover on it, to facing it against the walls, to putting Styrofoam padding in front of the speakers.

GW Were you playing the homemade, one-pickup guitar at this point?

VAN HALEN Not right in the beginning. I used to play a Les Paul and a 335, or whatever guitar I had at the time. I also played a Les Paul Junior. That was around the time I got a Strat and the guys didn't like it—"Sounds too thin." I said, "Okay, I'll take care of that." I slapped a humbucker in there and figured out how to wire up the rest of the stuff.

GW So the idea for putting a humbucker in a Stratocaster body came about as a matter of necessity?

VAN HALEN Oh, yeah. I just chiseled a hole in the body. I think I might even have some footage from the Whisky, where I played that original Fender Strat. It isn't the same one that appears on the first album. It's when I realized, Hey, this is neat, and got one from Charvel that was actually a Lynn Ellsworth guitar.

GW Had you seen or heard anyone reworking guitars like this?

VAN HALEN No. I hadn't really seen or heard anyone taking any time to try keeping a vibrato bar in tune either. A friend brought over a bootleg album of Hendrix in concert where he'd grab the bar, and the rest of the night it was out of tune. It was important for me, because for a long time before the Floyd Rose was developed I used a regular Fender vibrato. If you see the guitar on the first album cover there's no Floyd Rose. I actually did the first world tour with that guitar.

GW How did you keep it in tune?

VAN HALEN That's a tough one to explain. Due to the tension between the nut and the tuning peg, if you bring the angle of the string down it gets stuck in the nut. So I got a brass nut with extra big grooves and no string retainers, and I used to stick the string into the Schallers and wind it upward so the angle would be straight. I'd oil the brass nut, stick the string through the body, wind it a few times and then turn the ball end of the string, because when you tighten a string, you get tension along the string itself. I'd turn the ball so it was straight. That was just another thing in my mind that could cause a rubber band effect—where you loosen a string and it wouldn't come back to where it was. It's hard to say how much any of this had to do with it because certain strings would still go out of tune—they'd go sharp because they'd get caught up somewhere. So you'd have to go and snap it back before you hit the next chord. The thing is, I never hit all six strings when I play a chord; I'm usually doing some take-off on a chord, somehow.

I did this other thing once with a 335. They used to have a real cheap spring metal—bending vibrato on them; SGs had it too. I sawed my 335 in half because I figured I could always land on my feet and make it through a song barre-chording with the low E, A and D strings. So when I hit the vibrato bar it would only be for the high E, B and G strings. It worked great, it was neat. The three high strings would always be out of tune, and the low ones would always be in so I could always chord my way through, somehow. But the guys thought the 335 looked like something Johnny Rivers would play. I actually did that before I got a Strat. I did everything to that 335—belt-sanded it, repainted it, refretted it.

GW When you changed from the Gibson to the Fender, did your style alter?

VAN HALEN I never understood that. What's the difference? One less fret? I can get used to anything. I remember when I got a Strat, everyone was saying, "Oh, going to make it hard on yourself, huh?" Because people like Ritchie Blackmore would say things like, "I play a Fender because it's not the pussy way, it's not easy to play." I made it as easy as a Gibson to play. I never understood why Fenders are harder to play, except possibly that the string length is longer. I never tuned standard anyway, so that relieved a little tension. Try to play to the first record. We tune to A—or somewhere around there. I never tuned; if you can find a strobe-tuner in this studio I'll give you anything you want out of here. I'd just pick up the guitar and, whatever it was tuned to, I'd just tune the instrument to itself and have Mike tune to me, and we'd tune the synthesizer to it. Who made up the rule that an A string had to vibrate at 440, or whatever?

GW Who made the body of your first guitar?

VAN HALEN Boogie. I painted it almost immediately, because it was a wooden body, no finish. It was a junky, piece-of-shit body on the bottom of a stack of other bodies. It was a second. I gave the guy $50 and got a [*Boogie*] neck for $80. I picked up the body and neck and slapped it together; it's not that difficult.

GW What kind of guitar sound did you hear?

VAN HALEN I guess a cross between a Gibson and a Fender—a humbucker sound with a vibrato. Bigsbys were totally childish things. You couldn't really use them to bend pitches; they were a vibrato type of thing. What I wanted to do was fall off the edge of buildings.

GW Did you install Gibson frets?

VAN HALEN Yeah. I got the fret wire from Lynn Ellsworth and slapped them in. He told me how to do it. A couple popped up here and there so I got out the Krazy Glue.

GW Do you remember the first time you played the guitar after it was assembled?

VAN HALEN Yeah, it was neat. I thought, You can't buy one of these! I felt like I was onto something, and obviously I was.

GW Why just one pickup?

VAN HALEN In a two-humbucker–style Gibson, in order to get a clean, bright front pickup [*neck position*] sound, you'd have to sacrifice the sound of the rear pickup. I couldn't get what I wanted out of the front pickup, and I didn't feel like compromising, so I tended to stick with the rear one. And I tried to make up for a different sound color with playing techniques.

GW You used this guitar for the first tour?

VAN HALEN Before the first tour—during the Starwood and Whisky days. That was a couple of years before the first album.

GW Had you always used Marshalls?

VAN HALEN I tended to blow them up, so I used an old white Bassman or Bandmaster through a Marshall cabinet. I can't remember.

GW Were you using pedals?

VAN HALEN Same thing as on the first three tours: MXR flanger, MXR phaser and an Echoplex.

GW What was that hollowed-out bombshell you had onstage?

VAN HALEN That's what I used for the tail end of "Eruption." It was a Univox echo chamber. It had a miniature eight-track cassette in it, and the way it would adjust the rate of repeat was by the speed of the motor, and not by tape heads. So if you recorded something on the tape, the faster you played the motor back the faster it would repeat. And vice versa. I liked some of the noises I got out of them, but their motors would always burn out. I don't know how many broken ones I have. Then they stopped making them.

GW What were the first tours like?

VAN HALEN We went out with Sabbath, Ronnie Montrose, Journey. We did Day on the Green [*in Oakland*] with everyone from AC/DC to Foreigner. It was a hell of an experience.

GW Were you playing well then, by your own standards?

VAN HALEN Yeah, I think so. I wasn't ashamed of my playing. I didn't feel I had a lot to learn. I had a lot to learn about dealing with people, but I felt we held our ground pretty well. If anything, we took a little too much ground. Unintentionally. We didn't think, Hey, we're the best. We just did our gig and whatever happened, happened. Everyone else was a victim of his own bullshit. It didn't come from us.

GW What was it like, recording the first album?

VAN HALEN We didn't have a whole lot to say about much of anything. The songs basically got recorded the way we played 'em. Very few overdubs. I guess it was Ted's idea to make it come off as pure and simple and honest as it was live.

GW Did you agree with that?

VAN HALEN I wasn't sure. By the time Donn got through with it, I really liked it. I didn't know what making a record was. I guess it was good that we did approach it that way, because when we played live, you were only going to get more.

GW Did the songs on the first album mirror what you'd been playing live?

VAN HALEN Yeah. Things like "Ain't Talkin' 'Bout Love" and "Jamie's Cryin' " weren't on the original demo.

GW Had you been playing "Eruption" live?

VAN HALEN Yeah. Ted heard me practicing it for a Whisky show while I was waiting and he asked, "What's that?" I just didn't think it would be something we'd put on a record. He liked it, Donn liked it, and everyone else agreed that we should throw it on. I played it two or three times for the record, and we kept the one which seemed to flow. I like the way it sounds; I've never heard a guitar sound like it. It's not that my playing was so great, it just sounds like some classical instrument. Donn really made it sound like more than it is, in a way.

GW Were there any other songs you recorded which didn't make it onto *Van Halen*?

VAN HALEN "Loss of Control," which ended up on *Women and Children First*. We wrote "Loss of Control" and "Ain't Talkin' 'Bout Love" at the same time; we were actually making fun of punk rockers. "Ain't Talkin' 'Bout Love" was actually a stupid thing to us, just two chords. It didn't end up sounding punk, but that was the intention.

GW I suppose "Loss of Control" wouldn't have fit on the first record. It was pretty different.

VAN HALEN [*laughs*] You said it, not me!

GW Had you been in a studio prior to the first album?

VAN HALEN We were in the studio once before, with [*Kiss bassist*] Gene Simmons. That was about a year before.

GW What did you learn from that experience?

VAN HALEN I learned that I didn't like overdubbing. Gene naturally assumed I knew that was how it's done. Ordinarily, I would noodle between chord lines, and I had to fill in those rhythm spots on the tape. And I'd say, "Oh, I can't do that, I have to stick to this." So it was rather uncomfortable. When we got in the studio with Ted and Donn, I asked them if it would be okay to play the way I do live. And they said, "Sure, make it easier for all of us."

GW Prior to going into the studio with him, had you heard any of Ted's work?

VAN HALEN The first Montrose album; that was about it. Before we went into the studio to do the first album, we did a demo tape for Warner Bros. with Ted and Donn. There were 30 songs on it, and afterward we picked songs from those for the first album. We did the 30 songs in one day, and the next day, Dave, Mike and I put down the vocals. But after we did that demo tape we came up with other songs, like "Ain't Talkin' 'Bout Love." So since we'd done a demo tape, it was easy doing the record because it was the same setup and same way of recording. As a matter of fact, we have a bunch of songs from that tape we still haven't done. But they were written then, and I think I write better now. "House of Pain" was on that tape, and that just ended up on the last album [1984]. Some of the other titles were "Babe Don't Leave Me Alone" and "Peace of Mind." Good tunes, but, Van Halen–wise, kind of dated. They're a little dumber rock.

GW Whose idea was it to use Sunset Sound, the studio where the first albums were recorded?

VAN HALEN Donn and Ted had basically done all the Doobie Brothers stuff there; it was one of their favorite places. I didn't know anything about studios, so wherever they wanted to go was okay.

GW What was the first song you recorded?

VAN HALEN I don't remember. "On Fire," I think. I played the harmonics at the beginning on the A and D strings, one fret down from the E position [*seventh fret*] on the A string. It's actually not a harmonic; it's just a muffled, dead, weird sound. It sounded kind of machine-like. We wanted a little break between verses, and I said, "This is neat, how about this? It sounds rude."

GW Did you use a sitar on "Ain't Talkin' 'Bout Love"?

VAN HALEN I doubled that one part. It could have been a Coral guitar, but it looked real cheap. It looked like a Danelectro with some kind of stuff muffling the strings back there. I never really knew it was an electric sitar, because it didn't sound like one. It just sounded like a buzzy-fretted guitar. The thing was real bizarre.

GW How did you get that swishing sound on the intro to "Atomic Punk"?

VAN HALEN I used an MXR Phase 90 and rubbed my palm over the pickup. And then during two of the breaks I used a MXR flanger.

GW You used MXR pedals from the beginning?

VAN HALEN Yeah. I don't really use them anymore. I just use an Echoplex.

GW The guitar shown on the cover of the first album is the one you built?

VAN HALEN It's the same guitar I used on all the albums, and all the tours up until the *1984* tour. It was my baby until I started using the

Kramers. For a while I was putting Kramer necks on that main guitar [*pictured on the* Van Halen *cover*]. For the second album, I had that black and yellow guitar [*pictured on the back cover*].

GW Why did you change your guitar?

VAN HALEN I don't know why I played that black and yellow one. I liked the way it looked, but I didn't like the way it sounded. Actually, I used an Ibanez Destroyer for a lot of *Van Halen*—the guitar that is on the *Women and Children First* cover. On all the stuff that didn't have any vibrato on it, I used the Ibanez. "You Really Got Me," the rhythm track of "Jamie's Cryin' " and "On Fire," too. It has a PAF on it. It was one of the few guitars made out of Korina wood that you could get, without spending an arm and a leg for an original "V" or something. It was a great-sounding guitar—until I took a chunk out of it to make it look nice, to make it look different. On the cover of *Women and Children First*, it's missing a piece. Boy, did I screw it up.

"It bummed me out that Ted wanted our first single to be someone else's tune."

GW It changed the sound?

VAN HALEN Oh, completely. It ruined it. [*laughs*] It went from sounding like a nice, fat, warm guitar to "What the hell happened?" I couldn't believe it. The sound changed from a fat, Les Paul–type sound to a real weak Strat sound. I thought I'd ruined the pickup when I took the chunk of wood out, so I stuck in another pickup. But it sounded the same—real bad. I think it was because I took the wood out right by the bridge; that's where a lot of resonance and tone come from.

GW What is that story about Angel almost releasing "You Really Got Me" before Van Halen did?

VAN HALEN Yeah. A couple of guys from Angel were friends, acquaintances. One day—I forget where we were, it might have been the Rainbow—I was braggin' about our album, saying, "Hey, this is bad, you ought to listen to this." Because they had been talking about their new stuff. So we went up to [*drummer*] Barry Brandt's house, and they were all blown away by the album. They were all listening very carefully to this and that, and I left there feeling real good and proud. The next morning Ted Templeman called me up and said, "Did you play that tape for anybody?" And I said, "Yeah, I played it for all kinds of people!" He was pissed. I didn't know, nobody told me not to play it for anyone. I guess they figured I knew. And he said, "You asshole, why did you do that?" Because through the grapevine, Ted heard that Angel went into the studio and was trying to put out a single of "You Really Got Me" before us.

GW That really wouldn't have changed anything...

VAN HALEN I think it could have hurt. [*laughs*] So we released it as soon as possible—even before the album was out, I think. We had performed that song live for years. When we recorded demo tapes with Ted and Donn, that was actually the last song we did. Ted said then, "Well, you got anything else?" And we said, "Well, we've got some cover tunes." He said, "Play 'em."

It kind of bummed me out that Ted wanted our first single to be someone else's tune. I would have maybe picked "Jamie's Cryin'," just because it was our own.

GW Did the success of "You Really Got Me" lead to your doing another cover for the second album?

VAN HALEN I don't know how "You're No Good" came about. I guess it was Ted. He figured, "Hey, it worked the first time, let's try it again." I really don't remember how it ended up being picked. I didn't even remember how the damn song went. We used to play it in the bars, at Gazzarri's, but we didn't play it like that. We played it like the original [*Linda Ronstadt*] record. I know how this version came about, but I don't know how it came about that we used the song. Ted hummed the tune to me, and that's how I came up with the riff; I was just trying to noodle my way through it to figure out the chords. We never listened to the record to learn it. So I don't know if it's right or not.

GW Was "Spanish Fly" designed to follow-up "Eruption"?

VAN HALEN Al and I spent New Year's Eve, 1979, over at Ted Templeman's house. He had an acoustic guitar sitting in a corner, and I picked it up. I was getting drunk—and started playing it. I remember Ted saying, "Wow!" You can play acoustic guitar too?" And I said, "Yeah, I guess. It has six strings. It's not really any different." And I started doing hammer-ons—whoever came up with that name, hammer-ons?—and I started doing that stuff on the fingerboard and Ted said, "Hey, why don't you do something for the next record on acoustic guitar?" And I said, "Okay, sure." I bought a nylon-string Ovation and used it for that, and I don't know what happened to it. It took two or three takes.

GW Do you remember when hammer-ons became part of your style?

VAN HALEN I think it was around the end of the Gazzarri's days.

GW Had you heard of anyone playing like that?

VAN HALEN Honestly, no. I'm sure people had but I'd never seen anyone.

GW The sound of the bass on the first two albums seemed to be a little buried.

VAN HALEN I guess the sound Mike was getting at the time was either smothering everything if it was too loud or impossible to hear if you put it where it fit.

GW Did you suggest bass parts?

VAN HALEN Some things would just obviously follow the guitar-type of stuff, unless I had a specific bass line. Otherwise, Mike does whatever he feels like doing.

GW Moving on to *Women and Children First*, did the album mark the first time you used a keyboard in the studio?

VAN HALEN Yeah, on "And the Cradle Will Rock..." I had an old Wurlitzer electric piano and I pumped it through my Marshalls. A lot of people don't even know that because it doesn't really sound like a keyboard. That was my first encounter with the band not wanting me to play keyboards—when we did the song live, Mike played it. They didn't want a "guitar hero" playing keyboards, and that kind of ties in with why they didn't want "Jump."

GW Did you think about staging a keyboard-oriented song?

VAN HALEN Yeah. I saw no harm in my playing keyboards, as long as I do it well. I still think I should have played "And the Cradle Will Rock..." live because Mike is not as much of a keyboard player as I am. He can be taught, like anybody can, but since I played it on the record and wrote it, I figured I could play it a little better.

GW Did you put an effect on the Wurlitzer for the record?

VAN HALEN I just banged on the lower part of the keyboard—no notes, just a cluster—and switched on my MXR flanger.

GW The break in "Romeo Delight" had a real Who-type feel to it. Were you aiming for a *Live at Leeds* quality?

VAN HALEN It just kind of happened. I never try to get a certain kind of feeling. I just try to get any type of feeling at all—whatever comes out. [*laughs*] Whatever came out is the feeling I got.

GW There's also a heartbeat sound on "Romeo Delight."

VAN HALEN I think Mike was picking quietly, and I tapped my string against the pickup poles.

GW Was that the Stratocaster?

VAN HALEN I think that was the Ibanez. I butchered it for the photo session after the record was recorded. [*Sometime after this conversation took place, Edward remembered borrowing an Ibanez Destroyer from Chris Holmes of W.A.S.P. and using it for portions of the* Women and Children First *album.—Ed.*]

GW At the beginning of "Fools," you play some Eric Clapton–style blues.

VAN HALEN Yeah; I don't know where that came from. I think it was Ted's idea to get Dave's voice to sound that way. He wanted people to hear a different side of Dave's voice. That backup kind of blues guitar seemed to fit. That was the Ibanez.

GW There are all kinds of effects happening in the intro of "Everybody Wants Some!!"

VAN HALEN I did kind of a cello thing on the low E string with the palm of my hand. It's the same technique used on "Atomic Punk," but I'm not hitting all the strings.

GW Did you double the rhythm part to get that fat sound on "Everybody Wants Some!!"?

VAN HALEN No, I've never doubled a rhythm part. I don't know, I just turn it up, I guess. Everything is on 10. We just use cheap Shure 57s.

GW What is the effect on the guitar on "Tora! Tora!"?

VAN HALEN That's backward, and we kicked an Echo Plate [*EMT*] at the end of it. Just for fun.

GW What kind of acoustic guitar do you play on "Take Your Whisky Home"?

VAN HALEN I don't know what that was; just a rented job.

GW Do you enjoy playing acoustic guitar?

VAN HALEN Not really. It's not loud enough.

GW Isn't there also an acoustic on "Could This Be Magic?"

VAN HALEN Yeah, and I played slide on that for the first time in my life. It was kind of funny. Dave and I played together, and I don't know, I guess we had a little difference in rhythm. Like on "Ice Cream Man," Dave played the guitar, that little acoustic part. I just used some glass job for the slide. I had listened to Duane Allman a little bit on *Layla*, but slide is something that has never really interested me. I played in standard tuning.

GW What is that little piece of music that just fades into nothingness at the very end of side two?

VAN HALEN It was something Al and I were working on. I forget what we called it—"Growth," or something like that. We thought that just for the hell of it we'd stick it at the end of the record. And possibly start the next record with it. But it never amounted to anything, so we left it at that.

GW To my mind, *Fair Warning* took Van Halen to a higher level in terms of record production. There were more guitar parts and more textures. Is that accurate?

VAN HALEN I guess. I remember I approached my playing a little differently, where almost every song had an overdub in it, whereas before it was kept way down to a minimum. I wrote rhythm parts that I intended to solo over.

GW Are you able to hear in your head what the various parts will sound like when they're finally put together?

VAN HALEN Yeah, I usually can tell, but sometimes what I hear in my head doesn't work. But the majority of the time it does.

GW You did some of the writing for *Fair Warning* on piano?

VAN HALEN I did some stuff on piano and some stuff that still hasn't been used—obviously. [*laughs*] The album took a long time to record, because I was getting married and this and that. In the same way *1984* took the longest because the US Festival got in the way. We'd start to record, and then we'd have to make a radio program, etc. Every time we'd start to record it was [*in nasal voice*], "Oh, yeah, we forgot to tell you, you owe us this by tomorrow." The US Festival was actually like a whole tour's worth of work for one hour of playing— everything from the stage setup to rehearsing for it to all the video stuff that we owed them. I know Donn and I were happy to wash our hands clean of that when it was done.

GW It didn't seem to mar the success of *1984* at all.

VAN HALEN No, it didn't. But if we would have had to have the record out at a certain deadline in the middle of that, it would have suffered. But we said, "Screw 'em. We'll put it out when it's damn well ready."

GW What is the technique you use at the beginning of "Mean Street"?

VAN HALEN I tapped on the 12th fret of the low E and the 12th fret of the high E, and muffled both with my left hand down by the nut. I got kind of a funk slap out of the guitar. I applied to guitar what bass players do when they slap. But it's not like I studied it or anything.

GW The solo on "Mean Street" was very aggressive. Were you an angry young man that day?

VAN HALEN [*laughs*] I wasn't trying to be mad, but it just seemed to fit. I think I did do some interesting solos on the *Fair Warning* album.

GW You decided to try your hand at slide again on "Dirty Movies."

VAN HALEN I came up with the melody of it on slide, so I played it on the record on slide. The funny thing was I couldn't get up high enough on the guitar, so I sawed part of it off. I used an old Les Paul

Junior that had an SG body style and that one hook...what do you call it?

GW Horn?

VAN HALEN Horn. Yeah, the bottom one was in the way, so I took a hacksaw right there in the studio and said, "Hold this, Ted," and sawed it off.

GW The bass sound on *Fair Warning* was much better than it was on the previous records.

VAN HALEN Yeah. We used different amps, smaller amps—smaller amps usually get a better bass sound.

GW Didn't you do something interesting with the solo in "So This Is Love?"

VAN HALEN Out of six solo tracks, Ted let me mess around a little bit, but I don't think he thought I could get anything. Then Donn showed up and said, "Why don't you try it once?" I thought I was just trying it, but he recorded my composite and that was my first attempt. It's like four solos punched together. That surprised a few people.

GW Do you go through different feels for a solo before coming up with one that you think will work?

VAN HALEN I don't know. It's not an intentional, planned-out thing. Whatever sounds right, I guess.

GW Do you know if it's right when you hear it back?

VAN HALEN Yeah. Obviously, you'd better know if it's right when you hear it back. If not, you're up the creek.

GW "Sunday Afternoon in the Park" was another song that featured synthesizer.

VAN HALEN It was one of those cheap little kid's toys, an Electro Harmonix. It didn't have any notes; you could rub your hand across the whole octave of the board and it would go *rrrrrrrrrrrrr* [*rolls* *tongue and imitates sequencer line].* I just blazed it through the Marshalls. It was cheaper than a Casio, and was made of cardboard, plastic and a little sensor keyboard.

GW Could this have been the seed for "Jump"?

VAN HALEN As a matter of fact, I might have had "Jump" by then.

GW You approached the tracks on *Diver Down* differently than you did those of the first four albums.

VAN HALEN Basically, we did more finishing up of individual tracks before moving on to the next.

GW You did four cover songs on *Diver Down.*

VAN HALEN That was too many—four too many. Dave always wanted to redo "Dancing in the Streets," and I remember him giving me a tape of it. I said, "I can't get a handle on anything out of this." I didn't want to do it, I didn't like it. So I suggested "Pretty Woman," because that seemed more a Van Halen song to cover. It was us. I was working on something on the Mini-Moog, and Ted happened to hear the riff and said, "Wow, we can use this for "Dancing in the Streets." So Ted and Dave were happy—and I wasn't. Because the riff I had for something else got used for a song I didn't even want to do.

GW You used a Moog for that song?

VAN HALEN A Mini-Moog with a delay set so it would go [*sings rhythm of song*]. It wasn't a sequencer; I've never used a sequencer.

GW Have you studied the workings of synthesizers to learn what they can really do?

VAN HALEN Only sound-wise. Not to the extent of most people. I don't know crap about 'em, really. I can play keyboards, and I twist the knobs until I get the sound that I like.

GW Did guitar synthesizer ever interest you?

VAN HALEN No. For many people it's a good instrument because they play guitar and don't play keyboards. But I figure, if you play keyboards, why bother having to change the way you play guitar in order to adapt to that? I prefer playing keyboards if I'm going to play synthesizer.

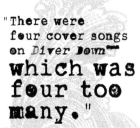

"There were four cover songs on *Diver Down* **which was four too many.**"

GW Were you using the Kramers for this record?

VAN HALEN I've never used a Kramer on record. I only got them for the *1984* tour. I may have put a Kramer neck on the guitars.

GW What attracts you to the Kramer?

VAN HALEN I just like their guitars. I play one all the time now, for recording and everything. The stuff I did for the *Wild Life* film was all on the Kramer.

GW You used a Fender Stratocaster on "Cathedral."

VAN HALEN Yeah, with an echo setting similar to that of "Dancing in the Streets," except it was a little slower so you could get that arpeggiated sound.

GW And you played a 12-string on "Secrets"?

VAN HALEN Yeah, one of those Gibson double-neck jobs. They were too heavy. I played it live and my shoulder was aching afterward. No wonder Jimmy Page has a slouch.

GW How did people react to "Secrets"?

VAN HALEN I thought it was a great song. It was different for us. Not for the sake of being different, but since we have something different we might as well stick it out there. I think that should have been the single before "Dancing in the Streets." But somehow it just got lost in the shuffle.

GW What guitar did you use on "Little Guitars"?

VAN HALEN We were on tour in Memphis during *Fair Warning*, and, sitting on the steps outside the hotel was a kid named David Petschulat, who stopped me and said, "Here, Eddie, check this out." And I went, "Wow." It was a perfect replica of an older Les Paul, except it was one third the size. I tripped, it was neat. So I took it to sound check and plugged it in. It sounded like a normal guitar, except higher in pitch. I started playing around on it and came up with the music for "Little Guitars." Later on, [*ZZ Top guitarist*] Billy Gibbons gave me a couple of those little Chiquita jobs, but I never really played them.

GW Which brings us to the *1984* album. If *Van Halen, Van Halen II* and *Women and Children First* represent the first phase of the band's development, and *Fair Warning* and *Diver Down* represent the second level, then *1984* surely must be the third phase?

VAN HALEN In a way, it's Phase One of Donn and Ed. Donn and I were very involved in this record. We almost took control, to a point, because it was done here in our studio, and we knew what we wanted. We weren't about to let the album be puked out in any way—especially since it was done here. We wanted it to be an accurate representation of the sound of this studio, and in a way I guess we were proving ourselves—to ourselves, more than anybody. I think everything sounds the best; I like it all.

GW Did you play any other guitars besides the Stratocaster?

VAN HALEN I used a Gibson Flying V on "Hot for Teacher" and "Drop Dead Legs." Actually, I've used a lot of different guitars, recording-wise, but live I usually use just one. I used the V because I needed the pickup switch to do the quiet part in "Hot for Teacher." Live, I used a Roland echo box with a volume knob on it, and I hooked it up to my pedal boards so I could hit the pedal and drop the volume, because I couldn't reach for the knob quick enough on the guitar. That song was beyond any boogie I've ever heard. It was pretty powerful.

GW *1984* was the first album in which you used the Ripley stereo guitar [*an instrument built by Steve Ripley in which each string can be sent to different sides of the speakers through the use of individual string pan pots*].

VAN HALEN I used that on "Top Jimmy." It's not really a stereo guitar; it has an individual pan pot for each string, so you can designate where each note you're playing will come out in the stereo spectrum. And I panned each string opposite each other, so the low E string would come out way left and the A string would come out right in the stereo picture. We used it on another thing, called "Ripley," that we didn't use on the record. It's a great guitar—a different guitar. You need two amps for it. There's another one that has built-in vibrato, and is actually like a miniature console with send and receive effects, and a patch bay where you can put a different effect on each string. I haven't gotten into that, but I can just imagine having a different effect on each string, panning it wherever you want, and adding vibrato to it. It's basically a guitar for the Eighties—or Nineties.

GW Weren't you toying around with the idea of building your own amplifier for production?

VAN HALEN Jose Arredondo, who works on my amps, and I had some ideas of building our own and selling it as my amp. It'll definitely be an amp that sounds the way I want it to. It will have everything you could possibly want in an amp for good sound.

GW Getting back to the *1984* album, what keyboard did you use for "Jump"?

VAN HALEN I used an OBX-A. They stopped making them, so now I play an OB-8, which is a better keyboard. You can basically get the same sounds out of it; there's just a slight difference between the two. To my ears, the OBX-A seems to have a little warmer sound, but the OB-8 is much more dependable.

GW So you were fiddling around in the studio—hearing a sound and thinking that it would be right for the song?

VAN HALEN Yeah. I just knew what sound I wanted to noodle with; not necessarily for "Jump," but just to noodle with. Whenever I sit down, I know what kind of sound I'm looking for.

GW You've described your guitar sound as the "brown" sound. What color is your keyboard sound?

VAN HALEN The same. Brown. I play brown to drums, everything. It's just a warm sound. Warm, big, majestic.

GW Did you wonder what guitar fans would think about your playing keyboard?

VAN HALEN No; I think the band wondered about it. I think as long as you do something well, what's the difference? I just knew that everyone from my father to the guy who works on my cars loved it. It had a universal appeal to it. If people didn't like it, that's fine, too. I knew what it was. Donn and I liked it so much, we didn't care what anybody else thought about it, I guess.

GW Were there many takes before the final version?

VAN HALEN I think we just did it once. Actually, the tape ran out at the very end, just in time. That's why we had to be careful with the fade at the end. When Donn mixed it, he had to fade it just right; otherwise he would have run out of tape.

GW Did you play the keyboard on the basic track?

VAN HALEN Yeah, we were all out there at the same time, and then I put the guitar on. The guitar at the end of the song was actually another song. We laid down that other track, too. Also, we were going to redo "In the Midnight Hour," but ended up not using it. The solo in "Jump" was spontaneous; I don't know if it was a first take.

GW Your main contribution to the *1984* album was as keyboardist. Any thoughts on that?

VAN HALEN No. [*laughs*] It's neat. It's almost like I play more keyboards now than I do guitar. I enjoy playing keyboards. It means you don't have to jump around onstage and have something hanging round your neck. No, I'm joking.

GW Did the overall success of *1984* give the band more freedom to wander outside the boundaries?

VAN HALEN It gave me the freedom to play keyboards comfortably. Now I don't have to worry about what the rest of the guys think other people will think. I never worried about what anyone thinks, except it makes you feel kind of uncertain when the guys worry.

GW Did you think about staging "Jump" live?

VAN HALEN No. I just figured I'd cut the solo out because it's such a short little thing, or play it on keyboard, which I did. Mike played a Mini-Moog bass live, since I did some counter-melodies on the record that I didn't have enough hands for.

GW "I'll Wait" was another keyboard song.

VAN HALEN That was one they really didn't want. It was actually that, more than "Jump," they didn't want to touch with a 10-foot pole. So Donn and I basically did the track with Al. Ted and Dave didn't like it.

GW Where did the song "1984" come from?

VAN HALEN The intro? That was the very first thing we ever did in this studio here. I was out there noodling on a synthesizer, and Donn was recording it without my knowledge. It was 45 minutes of me noodling like that. And we ended up using part of it.

GW Having 5150 must have opened up a new world for you.

VAN HALEN Oh, yeah. *1984* would not have been what it is if it wasn't done here.

GW What about some of the non–Van Halen projects with which you've been involved, like writing the music for *The Wild Life*?

VAN HALEN Donn and I saw the script for *The Wild Life* and said we'd do something for it. We ended up doing just about the whole film. It was fun, but we were kind of under pressure because of the deadlines. I had to leave to go on tour again, so I sort of left Donn to finish the mixing and everything. I played all the instruments.

GW How come there is only one song [*"Donut City"*] on the soundtrack album?

VAN HALEN We didn't really want anything on it. The songs on the record aren't even in the movie. We said that if they had to have something on the album, take "Donut City." We were concerned about doing stuff for the film, not selling a record.

GW And you did some music for Valerie's [*Bertinelli, Edward's wife*] film, *The Seduction of Gina*?

VAN HALEN Yeah, two songs. That was fun. Film music is much different than making an album. You sit there, watch the screen and think what would work.

GW What about the Brian May & Friends Star Fleet Project album?

VAN HALEN That was just a get-together jam. He invited me down to the Record Plant and we played. I didn't know he was planning to do a record. After we played, he called me up about four months later and asked what I thought about putting the stuff out. And I said, "Send me a tape, let me hear it first," because I didn't remember how it went. He did and I said, "Sure, what the hell." It reeks of fun. I broke a string in one of the blues jams and we just kept going; we didn't fix it. Brian is good. He gets a brown sound.

GW And you played on a Nicolette Larson album?

VAN HALEN Yeah, I played on one song. That was a favor for Ted.

GW Have you worked a long time at developing the brown sound?

VAN HALEN Not really. Yes and no. It's basically a tone, a feeling that I'm always working at. Everything is involved in that, and I've been working with it since I've been playing. It comes from the person.

GW Was the brown sound being developed when you were listening to Eric Clapton and learning all his solos?

VAN HALEN I don't know. It was always the live stuff I was into.

GW Could you listen to "Crossroads," for example, and pick out the solo note-for-note?

VAN HALEN Not that easily. Because the way Baker, Bruce and Clapton played live, those guys twisted and bent to the ultimate extremes of 4/4. There was something about them that I say about myself, though I'm not saying I'm in their league or bitchin' in that way at all, but they had a quality of falling down the stairs and landing on their feet. Listen to "I'm So Glad," on *Goodbye Cream*. Incredible, man! For my mind, nothing has matched it to this day. It was totally reckless-abandon-but-knowing-where-you're-goin'. People used to think I was nuts to sit there and listen over and over to what they would call noise. I don't even care if they knew what the other guy was doing. Going from total confusion to clicking together blew me away. I'm sure they weren't that good every night.

GW That's the key.

VAN HALEN Exactly. In a fun way, pushing yourself for yourself. Pushing yourself to a limit and taking a chance.

GW Does Van Halen take chances?

VAN HALEN Al and I do, all the time. Dave doesn't really like it and Mike isn't really plugged in with Al and me, so he kind of stops and lets us go crazy. Al and I just jam; sometimes we get carried away and go for too long, and we'll hear about it after the show. The next night we'll do it even longer! I'm joking. We don't do it on purpose; we do it because, to me, that's what making music is about. And that's what I always loved about Cream. They made music exciting in a way I don't think people really understood. It was almost as if the lyric and actual song structure was secondary. "Let's get this shit over with so we can make music and see where we land tonight." I loved that.

GW Have you done that on record?

VAN HALEN No. We've captured feelings to that effect but we've never put anything on record that is a jam, where somebody starts something, somebody follows and you work off each other. Al and I do that all the time by ourselves, but we've never put that on record because it's not a hit single. But who cares about a hit single?

GW Maybe that's where an album on your own might come in.

VAN HALEN Oh yeah, sure. But why even bother? Why not just do it and feel good about having done it?

GW You said earlier you weren't interested in hit singles. It seems you're sure that if you find enjoyment in it, other people wouldn't. That's not necessarily the case.

VAN HALEN That's true. But I guess I don't understand the rationale for putting something that personal out. And I guess Cream had more balls than I ever had. They did that and said, "Here we are." I guess the closest we've gotten to that is the first album, which was basically recorded live in the studio.

GW And that first album really captured a moment.

VAN HALEN It was different. But if the next album had been the same, then it wouldn't have been different, would it? It's very difficult to figure out what to do on record. Maybe that's why I haven't done

one on my own. I'm partly brainwashed by the whole aspect of the business—that there's something expected of me. What if I did something totally off the wall that I personally enjoyed, and people thought something weird about me? In a way, I guess, it's exposing a side of yourself that is very difficult to expect anyone to understand in the slightest way. I'd rather not even expose myself or that type of music to any attack. You know how sometimes you can do something just for fun and people take it like it's your statement? I guess I don't even want anything to do with that whole thing. Do you understand?

GW To me, "Jump" was taking a chance—a keyboard tune from the guitarist of the Eighties.

VAN HALEN "Jump" was not a spontaneous jam. What I was talking about was that live-Cream, spontaneous thing. For one, it would take somebody with a hell of a sense of humor, and they'd have to be a musician to even get anything out of it. I'm talking total darkness concerning format—no form, no song structure, nothing. Maybe someday... At the moment, I'm just writing. We're talking about doing another Van Halen album.

GW A live recording?

VAN HALEN No, I don't see the purpose.

GW What do you do when you're not in the studio?

VAN HALEN Sleep.

GW Would you like to have a family?

VAN HALEN Yeah, I'd love to have a family, but it's not really the right time in my life. Maybe within a year or two.

GW Would you want your child to be a musician?

VAN HALEN Sure, why not? Only if he wants to be; I wouldn't force him. I think he or she will be exposed to music in an unforced way, and it will be their own choice. Of course, I'll try exposing them to it.

GW You told me once that most of the music you hear on the radio sounds the same.

VAN HALEN Well, doesn't it? There's such a handful of heavy metal bands, that God, I can't tell the difference. There's no unique quality that sticks out in my ear. They all play as fast as they can, as loud as they can, scream as high as they can, but they don't even scream, or play fast, with a unique quality. They don't.

GW You also said some players do have good guitar sounds, but something is missing.

VAN HALEN Yeah. I don't know what it is. It leaves me cold. Obviously it doesn't leave everyone cold, because they sell records like hell. The state of rock and roll right now is like incest. You have bands that are clones, and you have bands who are clones of clones—and they all start copying each other to the point where it's like incest. And obviously you're going to have retarded kids. [*laughs*]

"It's definitely time to move on."

GW I asked you earlier if you wanted to be Beethoven. What about being a guitarist during the Sixties, playing alongside musicians like Page and Clapton?

VAN HALEN Yeah, I guess. It would have been fun.

GW If the moment had never arrived for you, would you be content still playing Gazzarri's?

VAN HALEN Yeah. I love making music just for the sake of doing it. My dad is starting to teach me how to play saxophone. I'd really like to get into that; I love saxophone. But it's tough, it's a hard instrument. For me it is, anyway. And I'm going to go out and buy a cello, too.

GW So for your solo record we can expect to hear a...

VAN HALEN A synthesizer-saxophone-cello-piano album. [*laughs*] We'll call it *Guitar? What Guitar?*

GW I just have a feeling that when we next hear Van Halen they won't be...

VAN HALEN The same? Maybe you're right. I guess we'll all have to sit around and wait, and see what that difference will be. I don't really know. It's definitely time to move on.

[8]

"Sammy bought a house two doors away from me and we get along great. It's like we've known each other all our lives, really. Very close."
—*EDDIE VAN HALEN*

ON THE ROAD

David Lee Roth was out, Sammy Hagar was in,
and *Guitar World* was there to get the inside
scoop from Eddie Van Halen.

BY STEVEN ROSEN

GUITAR WORLD You seem so happy with the new band.

EDWARD VAN HALEN Dave always said I'm not happy unless I'm unhappy, so to speak. And that's a crock—I'm happy as hell and I'm coming up with some great stuff.

GW Will you ever look back at those years with Dave and regret that it all fell apart?

VAN HALEN Hell no. It was a blessing in disguise. When we get nominated for a Grammy and win, I'm going to thank him. [*laughs*] I'm serious.

GW Have you heard any of the music Dave's been working on?

VAN HALEN I hear it's good. [*Bassist*] Billy Sheehan is a bad mother—one of the best around.

GW They may have songwriting problems—Dave doesn't write and [*guitarist*] Steve Vai doesn't write those types of songs.

VAN HALEN And Billy writes heavy metal riffs.

GW So he'll have to find outside writers.

VAN HALEN He already bought some tunes from Steve Lukather. Steve is such a nice guy, he actually asked me, "Hey, do you mind?" I said, "Hell no, I don't mind." Billy Sheehan kind of asked me the same thing. And I said, "What do you think? Dave just left the band and he wants the hottest guns in town to replace us." And he asked, "Well, hey, we're still friends, right?" And I said, "Sure, I don't care. I got no beef with you." Actually, I've got no beef with Dave either—it's just that he really hurt me. You know? That's what it boils down to, and that's why I was so pissed off in the very beginning. At the height of our career—you work at something for so long, and all of a sudden someone just pulls the plug on you. That's kind of cruel.

"Dave's a creative guy—but he's a lousy human."

GW Did Dave really pull the plug?

VAN HALEN Yeah, he quit! We weren't getting along, but we never did, basically.

GW Didn't you want to leave the band several years ago?

VAN HALEN Yeah, four years ago. During *Fair Warning*. I wanted to quit, but I stuck with it, and that's what burns my ass even more. If I would have quit then I wouldn't have spent an extra four years putting up with his attitude. I mean, hey, the guy's creative, okay? But he's a lousy human. Trying to live with the guy on tour...you ask anybody that's gone on tour with us, and they'll tell you he'd yell and scream for his apple in the morning. Or ransack people's rooms for the *Playboy* somebody borrowed the night before.

GW Power trips?

VAN HALEN Oh yeah. And Noel Monk [*the band's manager at the time*] was his goddamn puppet—did everything he wanted. And that's partly why Al and I wanted to change; we wanted a manager who managed the band—not someone who did only what one person said.

GW Had you left during *Fair Warning*, it would have been…

VAN HALEN …different, sure. Well, let's put it this way: The end result is, I'm very happy now. Whatever it took to get where I am now, I'm very happy.

GW Was "Dreams," from the new album, played on the MIDIed piano?

VAN HALEN Yeah, I think so. We never even got to work with Dave on that; we rehearsed maybe for a total of a week within a month's time.

GW So he had heard some of the new material?

VAN HALEN Oh yeah, I had "Good Enough" and "Summer Nights," and we'd begun work on "Dreams."

GW It appears from *5150* that your writing has moved in new directions.

VAN HALEN It's constantly changing, I guess. I don't really know where inspiration comes from—or where anything comes from.

GW Was there any worry about the ideas not being there?

VAN HALEN Oh, not at all. The way I feel about it is, Sammy and I are in tune with each other. I have to say that, often, opposites will attract. Dave and I were completely opposite in our backgrounds and music, our musical styles and what we enjoyed listening to. And sometimes that works. The friction creates something.

GW Like with the Who?

VAN HALEN Yeah, but there Pete Townshend writes everything. With Sammy, we're the same—and it seems to work better. So the theory that opposites attract is not valid in this case.

GW Did you listen to many singers before finding Sammy? I know you listened to [*Australian vocalist*] Jimmy Barnes.

VAN HALEN And he's doing well. I got a tape from him, and it's the same record he has out now. I don't know; he's a great singer, but I didn't think he was right for the type of music that I write.

GW Did you think that having Hagar in the band would make it sound like Sammy Hagar's band? As opposed to some unknown vocalist?

VAN HALEN I think Sammy Hagar's work on this record is like nothing he's ever done. No, I never thought we would sound like Sammy Hagar, because I'd be writing the music, and my music doesn't sound like Sammy Hagar music. I pulled some vocals out of him where even Sammy kind of flipped and said, "Whoa, I didn't know I could do that." I guess we pushed each other.

GW Was Mick Jones important in that area?

VAN HALEN I produced all the vocals with Sammy except for "Dreams," because Mick was on tour. Mick helped out a great deal in organizing things. You know how I am—"Hey, let's work on this today. Nah, let's work on that." Or whatever. He really helped pull it all together and polish it up, so to speak. Mick [*Jones, producer*] changed a few things and he offered a few ideas. He and I wrote "Dreams" with Sammy. The song was completely different than it is now. Originally, what is now the verse part was actually a part of the solo section. The same parts were still there but they were juggled around. And he tore a hell of a vocal out of Sammy on that one. Mick is great to work with, a nice guy. We call him "The Duke." A proper English guy.

GW How did you meet him?

VAN HALEN I met him through Sammy at the MTV Awards. Now, it's in our contract that Warner Bros. has the right to refuse producers. I wanted the band to do it by ourselves with Donn, and they said, "No." So what we did was, we went ahead and did the whole record anyway, and then brought Mick in and had him kind of oversee it. But I think Warner knows now that I'm not the flake that I've been reputed to be.

> "I built the 5150 studio for the benefit of all of us, for the family, for the band. But I guess certain people didn't look at it that way."

GW Billy Gibbons had a similar experience—no one was sure about the idea of bringing synthesizers into ZZ Top, and he just asked for a chance to be heard. I think they believe him now.

VAN HALEN Yeah. [*Warner Bros. production executive*] Lenny Waronker was a great help. He came down and heard stuff that we were doing, and he was flattened—floored. He said, "Whoa, I didn't think you guys could pull it off." After he heard a couple of cuts he said, "Go for it," even before Mick showed up. Then he began to trust us.

GW How come you're not working with Ted Templeman anymore?

VAN HALEN Actually, he came to one rehearsal. We showed him about four or five tunes. He made notes and everything, but he had a commitment to Dave. He didn't know when he was going to be working with Dave, and it just so happened that we wanted to start— we wanted to get rolling. I got sick of sitting on my ass. It's funny that Dave says we wanted to sit on our butts and stay at home and not tour and not work. I sat on my thumbs waiting for him for eight months, and I didn't want to wait another month to start recording. And Ted said, "I have a previous commitment," and we said, "Okay, fine, see ya later." It wasn't like we split. I'm not saying we'll never work with him again; it wasn't that type of thing. Ted is great, but he took Dave's side. But it was obviously because he committed himself to Dave after his *Crazy from the Heat* thing.

GW Perhaps Ted has more control over Dave than he does over you.

VAN HALEN Oh, sure, yeah. With us he'd have to put up with me. [*laughs*] Which I don't know if he's into too much.

GW Logistically, then, if Ted could have produced both the Roth and Van Halen albums, you would have agreed to that?

VAN HALEN [*pauses*] Probably, yeah...I don't know, it's hard to say. Put it this way, he was our number one choice because, obviously, he knows me and Alex and Mike and Sammy very well [*Templeman produced Hagar's* VOA *album and the Montrose records*]. And he and Donn have worked together for years. So it just seemed like a logical thing. Whatever differences there may have been, it could have worked. At least from my end.

GW I get the impression that you wanted to be more involved in *5150*.

VAN HALEN Oh, sure. The way we did this record is basically how I would like to have done all the previous ones. And I think that's another thing that maybe drove Dave away. For *1984*, I built the studio, and began wanting to do things a little more my way. I guess I turned some people off; I created a little friction, though unintentionally. I built the studio for the benefit of all of us, for the family, for the band. But I guess certain people didn't look at it that way, because Ted sure didn't dig working up there. Even though he loves the sound of the place, he just kind of looked at it like if I got pissed at him, I'd kick him out of my studio. [*laughs*] Though I'd never do that. If anything, Dave is the one who did that.

GW Do you wish you could've worked with Dave the same way you do with Sammy?

VAN HALEN I don't know. I don't know if I could have gotten out of Dave what I can get out of Sammy. I don't know if this is slandering Dave, but Sammy is just a better singer; he can do anything I ask him to do. Whereas Ted has a much better handle on what to get out of Dave, because Dave is kind of limited, vocally—range-wise and stuff. I don't know if that's a bad thing to say. I don't know how that is going to look in print. But I mean, hey, Dave has a unique voice and a unique style and also has a very strong idea of what he wants. So does Sammy, but I just pushed him a little further. Gave him a little confidence and said, "Hey, hit this note." And he'd go even higher than the note I asked him to hit. He'd be blown away and it would be great.

GW Did the fact that Sammy had greater facility than Dave lead to a change in your approach to writing songs?

VAN HALEN Sure. Like in "Why Can't This Be Love?" there is this part [*sings the middle part where the voice doubles the keyboard*]. I would never have attempted to ask Dave to do that.

GW The *5150* sessions felt good with Sammy?

VAN HALEN More than anything. He's changed my life. Seriously. He bought a house two doors away from me and we get along great. It's like we've known each other all our lives, really. Very close.

GW Why wouldn't Dave allow himself to be a friend?

VAN HALEN I don't know. Well, in the beginning I guess we were, kind of. But he was always too much into being a star. And that is what he is. I'm a musician, he's a star. A musician doesn't want to go and star, direct and write his own movie. We were really just different people. Sammy and I are a little more the same. A little more human, so to speak. [*laughs*]

GW Is the feeling in the band now similar to what you experienced during the very early days of Van Halen?

VAN HALEN Dave pretty much always had that edge to him—that attitude. I don't know where it came from—insecurity, or having to prove something to his peers. But he always had that uncomfortable kind of attitude of never letting his guard down and opening up and actually letting you inside him. Sometimes I wouldn't know what kind of mood he was in. He's so moody sometimes that you only converse when he wants to. Whatever. Not much more about him, okay?

GW Okay. Getting back to the music, did you really meet Sammy through Claudio [*Edward's and Sammy's mechanic, who is pictured at the outset of Hagar's "I Can't Drive 55" video*]?

VAN HALEN Yes. Claudio gave me his phone number. He's a friend; I hang out at his shop sometimes to talk about cars. And I told him, "Hey, man, our singer left, he quit." And he said, "Hey, well, I just talked to Sammy today and he's coming to town." So he gave me Sammy's number and I called him up.

GW What was Sammy's reaction to the call?

VAN HALEN He said, "Wow, this could be something!" He wanted to come down to meet us first and see what kind of condition we were in. Because he'd heard some horror stories about my being...way out there, a space case. And he came down and said everything he heard through—well, I won't name any names—but he said, "Man, what's with those people? Why are they talking dirt about ya?"

He came down with Ed Leffler, his manager. We said, "Hey, we want a band, we don't just want to do a project with you. We want you as a permanent member of the band." First we had a little business meeting, just because he wanted to know what we wanted—to see whether it was like the album he did with Neal Schon, or what. We told him we wanted a permanent member. He came down the next Monday and we jammed, and that was it. The first tune we did was "Summer Nights." And from then on it was just straight up. In 20 minutes we had a complete song.

GW Was the energy similar to the feeling on *Van Halen*?

VAN HALEN I can't compare two totally different worlds, totally different atmospheres. Better. In the very beginning, the first album, I was very intimidated by never having been in a studio—it was all new to me. I learned over the years what I want and how to get what I want.

GW *5150* sounds more crafted than I thought it would be; I expected it to be...

VAN HALEN Rawer?

GW But if you examine it, it is the next logical step up from *1984*.

VAN HALEN I wouldn't say more "crafted"; crafted, to me, sounds like put-together. I'd say it's a little more polished, a little shinier. But not for the purpose of being more mainstream; that just happened to be the music I wrote. And that's the way it transferred to tape. I'm not about to deliberately screw something up to give it an edge. Everything has that garage-band energy, but it's polished—we haven't lost that rock and roll soul.

GW Was it an easy album to make, in terms of putting the songs together and knowing when they were right?

VAN HALEN A breeze. Beautiful. We never put anything down and then decided to change it. We'd write a tune, put it down, and say, "Yeah, that's it." We might've edited a few spots if a part was too long, but the elements were there.

GW Some time ago, you said you knew that whatever you did would be judged by what you had done. Did this make you nervous when you were recording *5150*?

VAN HALEN Oh, sure, it gave us all a little more *ooomph*. Made us try a little harder.

GW With regard to the session, were the keyboard parts recorded before the guitars?

VAN HALEN Yes, I did all the keyboards first, alone, and then Al put down drums and Mike overdubbed bass. And then I overdubbed guitar. On "Love Walks In," I played by myself without a beat at all. Seriously. Ask Donn. It was tough for Al but I wasn't that far off. I wanted the chorus part to retard a little bit, and you can't do that with a click track—it would've sounded too robot-like. So Donn and I said, "Forget it, we'll just wing it," and Al managed to play to it. "Dreams" was done with a click track. I used an old 1912 Steinway seven-foot B Grand MIDIed to an Oberheim OB-8.

GW Is that an acoustic guitar at the beginning of "Dreams"?

VAN HALEN Yeah. It's a new Kramer Ferrington acoustic guitar with a thin body and an electric guitar neck on it. They sent me the first one. It sounded great, so I had to use it on something.

GW Did you use the Steinberger guitar on the album?

VAN HALEN Yeah, with the Trans-Trem. I used that on "Summer Nights" and "Get Up." It's an amazing guitar. You can hit a whole chord with a whammy bar and it will go up or down in tune with itself. So "Get Up" sounds like I'm playing slide, but I'm actually using the wiggle stick.

GW You were initially wary of the guitar, I understand.

VAN HALEN Well, that was because I'm used to a piece of wood, and this thing is like plastic. It was kind of alien to me. I had to change a few things to make it sound right. For instance, I had to use my amp differently—I had to use a bassier input. But I talked to Ned [*Steinberger*], and he made some different pickups. They're still EMGs, but they're a little warmer-sounding than the ones he sent to me.

GW I noticed that the solos on the record sound kind of angry.

VAN HALEN Angry? Maybe subconsciously, I don't know. But I think they're just sleazy. Kind of slimy-sounding—you never know where they're going to go. They just slip and slide. It's like the old "fall down the stairs and hope you land on your feet" thing. Whatever fits.

"Dave and I made a lot of good music together."

GW Yet the solo on "Love Walks In" is so lyrical.

VAN HALEN Yeah, I planned that out. I had a melody in my head and it happened to fit. So I said, "What the hell? I might as well use it."

GW Does Sammy play any guitar on *5150*?

VAN HALEN No, I played all the guitars. Live, though, he does the solos on the keyboard tunes.

GW Years ago, didn't Ted Templeman want Sammy Hagar to be Van Halen's singer?

VAN HALEN I remember hearing something like that. The thing is, Dave has always hated Sammy. I never understood why. We did some shows together—the Oklahoma Jam, and Anaheim Stadium with Black Sabbath and Sammy Hagar—and I always went over and said hi to Sammy because I dug him from his Montrose days. And Dave would always talk shit about him: "Ahhh, that little mother, he ain't got nothin' on me." And I'd wonder, Where's that even coming from? Why the animosity? And what Dave says is true—they never even met. Sammy never said a bad word about Dave until Dave started saying shit about him in the English press. I never knew where he was coming from; probably a slight case of jealousy.

GW I wonder what Van Halen would have been like with Hagar as the original singer?

VAN HALEN Ummmm, I can't speculate. Maybe Sammy would be doing a movie right now, and Dave would be in the band. [*laughs*] You never know. Seeing how Sammy is blonde, too, we—Alex [*Van Halen, drums*], Mike [*Anthony, bass*] and I—figured our purpose was to make lead singers into actors, movie stars. It's just a joke.

GW *5150* is your first Number One album—how does it feel?

VAN HALEN It shows me that music overpowers bullshit. Dave and I wrote a lot of good stuff and made a lot of good music together, but I guess the clowning and the show biz part of it only works and helps so much. What's on that tape is what counts. Bottom line. And our going Number One proves that.

GW Then you think that coming off a huge album like *1984* would not have ensured success had you made a poor album?

VAN HALEN It would have bombed. But I think we made a good record—a solid record. There's not a song on there I don't like. On previous records there were tunes like "Dancing in the Streets." Come on! That's not me. A funny thing, though: We've played it live—on guitar. Just for fun. We did that in South America when we toured. Maybe. If I'd played it on guitar on the record it would have been better. The riff on the record actually was taken from a song of my own, that I was in the midst of writing. Ted heard it and said, "Hey, let's use it for that."

GW Looking back, what moments stand out for you? Was *1984* one of the high points?

VAN HALEN It was both a very high and a very low point, emotionally, for me. Since it was recorded at my house, I got a lot of flak from producers and from Dave. In a way, that made me work harder and, in a way, it turned me off to working with those people. So what I did was work at night after everyone split, and then the next day play stuff for them. They're the type of people who, I guess, like to work from noon to 6 P.M., break for dinner, go to sleep at 11, and wake up at noon again. You know what I mean? I'm not that type of person. And they knew that all along. So I guess it scared the crap out of 'em when I built the studio. Because, hey, I'd wake up at five A.M. and want to play. If an idea pops in my head, I want to put it down. You don't put off an idea until tomorrow. I basically wanted to work when I wanted to work, or when I *could* work. I can't just flick a switch on like Dave obviously can. I can't do it that way—at least not creatively.

GW But after *1984* came out and they saw what you were capable of, wouldn't they allow you more control?

VAN HALEN I don't know. I think it scared them more. I don't think they were ready to work with me under those conditions again. I think it was that, along with getting rid of our manager, that made Dave just say, "Well, screw you guys, I'm taking off, too." But we didn't do anything wrong. Alex and Mike and I were just sitting there saying, "Whoa! I thought we were doing great. What the hell is going on?" Here was Noel, our manager, suing us. What happened was, he wanted to renegotiate. He sent us a letter saying, "I want more money." We said, "Let's negotiate," but he wouldn't accept our offer. So we didn't fire him, he quit. And since Dave and he were so tight, so to speak, when Noel split he must have really felt he had no more control over me, Alex and Mike. Particularly since Al and I started opening our mouths for a change and were sticking up for what we thought was right. *1984* proved we were right, and so did this new one—not that we were even out to prove anything.

GW *5150* has more keyboards than any album you've ever done, and it's been the most successful.

VAN HALEN And what's funny is that Dave was basically against keyboards. Like Billy Gibbons and his, "Hey, you're a guitar hero, nobody wants to see you play keyboards." They had a mental block.

We never even got together long enough to see what he would have come up with for the stuff I was writing. He was too busy doing interviews for his solo career when we had a record to make. He'd call up and say in a gravelly voice, "Ah, I can't make it today, man," and I'd call the office and he'd be doing interviews.

GW What did you think of *Crazy from the Heat*?

VAN HALEN I think it was a novelty item. He didn't write any of it—it's full of songs written by other people. In my mind that's an easy way out, because the songs he did have been hits already. Ted has always said, "Hey, when you redo a hit you're halfway there, because the song's been proven." But that's not my way of thinking; I like to do my stuff. That isn't to say I like my own stuff better. But if you have ideas, why be a bar band—why not take a shot at your own stuff? I had enough of playing other people's music in clubs for seven years. Now that I have the chance, I want to do my own now.

GW You made a Number One album with no videos.

VAN HALEN Yeah, that's true. The reason was that we didn't have time to do even one. And on top of that, my main reason was that since Van Halen used to do such extravagant, loony videos, I didn't want people judging the new face in the band and the new unit by what they saw on some script. I wanted people to see us as we are onstage first. After it was known what we were about, then we could goof off and do whatever we wanted in videos.

Warner Bros. and everyone else wants a video out of us. Our next single is going to be "Dreams." We won't have the time to do a video for that unless we do a live one, so that's probably what we'll have to do. Live is actually the best way to go—it presents us the way we are, not engaged in doing some goofy stuff. The goofy stuff is fun to do, but we didn't want people to get their first impression of us that way.

GW Do you see yourself doing some outside producing?

VAN HALEN Sammy asked me to produce his next solo album. And it's going to be fun. I dig working with Sammy, it's great. We come up with stuff so quickly, it's incredible. And he can step out a little and do all kinds of stuff—like writing folk tunes on acoustic guitar. Show a side of himself other than the Red Rocker.

GW Will the next album show that side?

VAN HALEN Yeah. One thing Sammy's record won't be is anything like Van Halen. I'm not going to write or play on it; I'll just produce. Because if I write and play, it would sort of sound like Van Halen. And it's not a Van Halen record. I don't want anyone to have the impression that it is—or that he left the band and we're looking for another singer.

GW Speaking of outside projects, did anything ever come of your desire to work with Pete Townshend?

VAN HALEN I feel really bad about that. I think Pete Townshend is really pissed off at me. We talked—actually he never called—but he sent telegrams. I tried calling him back, and he telegrammed to say he doesn't like to work in the States, that he wanted to work in England. That kind of threw me a curve, because I was kind of planning to do it in the studio at home. But that wasn't the main reason. He wouldn't have been able to start until November of last year because he was doing his book and his solo album [White City]. I was tired of waiting to do something. Also, here are Alex and Mike, who I love, and who are my friends, and who I've been with for years—I couldn't exactly just leave them out. Pete and I never really discussed how to approach the thing, whether it would be Alex and Mike and me or what. I just hope he's not mad at me because I never got hold of him to tell him, "Sorry, I can't do it." I lost his number. I tried to call Phil Chen, who originally got the number for me, and I lost his number, too. You know what a slob I am. I write something down on a matchbook and I light a cigarette and throw the pack away. So Pete, if you read this: I apologize.

GW Weren't you also trying to work with Patty Smythe?

VAN HALEN I actually hit her up to possibly join the band and be our lead singer. I just bounced the idea off her. She wasn't sure she could deal with three guys, or something along those lines. And she has a happening solo trip.

Another thing that was bounced around was doing a record with me writing all the music and getting different singers—Joe Cocker, Phil Collins, Mike Rutherford—a different vocalist on each track. But Alex talked me out of it. He said that would be just a one-shot project, and it made me realize, Yeah, I want a family, I want a solid thing.

The thing is, I never thought Dave would quit—I thought he'd wake up. The things that he said were so weird. He asked how long the album was going to take, his attitude was [*mimics sarcastic tones*], "Hey, man, I've got better things to do, how long is it going to take?" I told him to count on about a year from starting point to album release—writing for a couple of months, recording for three months, and then all the red tape crap of mastering, album covers, T-shirts and all that. And he put it in the press like I just wanted to rot in the studio for a year. We recorded this album in three and a half months—we started in November and by March were on tour for nine months. And he told the press that these so-called "married men" with their Lamborghinis didn't want to tour, but only wanted to do some summer shows. He was the one who suggested not doing a record and just cashing in on the summer circuit. And I said, "What? I don't want to go on tour without any record." He said, "Hey, man, it don't matter." I said we had to do a new record.

The thing is, he's more into money than I am. I'm into making music; I'm a musician. And I love people liking what I'm doing. He's the businessman, not me.

GW How has Donn responded to the new face?

VAN HALEN Actually, it was Donn who said, "This is it." Seriously, that one Monday night we jammed, we played for 20 minutes and Donn flicked the talk-back button and said, "I never heard you guys sound that good."

GW Even Michael and Alex's sound has improved.

VAN HALEN Oh, yeah, it's a new fire. I'm not saying we couldn't have done a good record with Dave, but I think he started believing the attitude he started copping, the "Hey, I'm God" syndrome. To the point where his hat wouldn't fit his head anymore. I was still willing to put up with it.

GW I'm curious: how did Valerie respond to all this?

VAN HALEN She was pissed off, too, because she knew I wanted to quit years ago when we were doing *Fair Warning*. He used to pull shit on her, telling me, "Tell your old lady not to say this and that in the press about you." Bullshit stuff. I said, "Hey, I'm normal, and whatever you are, you are. Don't tell my wife not to say the way I am." I could write a book about the stuff that went down, and none of it had anything to do with music. The guy just did not treat anybody like a human. He was like Idi Amin or Muammar Qaddafi.

[9]

"I don't please myself
very easily."
—*EDDIE VAN HALEN*

ED, EDDIE, EDWARD

Good buddy, guitar virtuoso, perfectionist:
three faces with a single purpose—producing
the Van Halen signature sound.

BY BUD SCOPPA

HE 5150 COMPLEX LIES at the end of a rutted private road, on a wooded hillside rising out of the San Fernando Valley. The hills here are swarming with rock stars, most of whom keep their gates closed. But not this rock star—not now, anyway. There's been a steady stream of traffic in and out of 5150 of late, and the guys in the clubhouse are too busy to be buzzing the gate open every 10 minutes. There are movies to watch on the big-screen TV, pinball games to be played on the Elton John *Captain Fantastic* pinball machine, video battles to be waged on *Asteroids*, *Tempest* and *Omega Race*, hoops to be shot at the NBA-approved basketball goal affixed to the wall of the studio ("Hey, man—keep that ball away from my Lamborghini—please!") and...oh, yeah, there's a Van Halen album to be finished, as soon as Ed, Al, Mike, Sammy, Donn and the guys who work for them get up to cruising speed.

Driving past the gate, you immediately notice that Van Halenland is divided into two distinct parts. On the right side of the driveway is Valerie Villa, with its impeccably maintained estate house, dark-blue-painted swimming pool, well-groomed pets and an air of understated elegance.

On the left side—further on up the road, as it were—is Boys Town, which houses the recording studio, with its myriad of manly diversions, discarded burrito wrappers and bunches of guys in various stages of busyness. Upstairs is the Edward Van Halen Guitar Showroom (formerly Mrs. Van Halen's exercise room). It's so jam-packed with axes and other weaponry that there just isn't enough room for all of it. Some of Eddie's junk—the guitar synth he never plays, for instance—lies abandoned in a corner. Within the messy confines of his citadel, Van Halen can be himself and do what he does best: write/arrange/produce/play rock and roll music, and be a regular guy—just like all the regular guys he surrounds himself with.

As I pull up to 5150 at high noon, Eddie Van Halen stands by the studio door, grinning that puckish, lopsided, puffy-eyed grin of his. He leads me into the control room, sits in a swivel chair and places an ashtray on the butt-strewn floor between us.

First things first: What does he like to be called?

"Ed, Eddie, Edward—I don't give a damn," he answers, punctuating his words with a snicker. "I used to care—I don't anymore. When I'd introduce myself to people as 'Edward Van Halen,' they'd go, 'Who?' So I'd go, 'Eddie Van Halen.' 'Oh, yeah, sure!' So a lot of times I call myself Eddie now. Al calls me 'Ed'; I call Al 'Al'; my mom calls him 'Alex'...I dunno."

Ed/Eddie/Edward laughs a lot, and his hands are always busy. When he talks about playing the guitar, his fingers move over invisible frets; when he makes a point, he taps you on the knee, good buddy-style. Not only does he play the guitar rhythmically, he moves and speaks according to some internally generated tempo. The guy emits a constant beat.

Van Halen seems entirely too unpretentious to be a mega-celeb—but then you realize that he has carefully arranged his world so that it is possible for him to behave approximately like a normal human being and do his work in surroundings he considers comfortable. Here's a man who can afford the lifestyle of the richest and most famous and he's chosen the clubby, chummy, sorta cruddy surroundings of his clubhouse. The studio is crammed with the most sophisticated audio gear on the planet, but there's a layer of dust and ashes over everything. Ed wouldn't have it any other way.

"Hey, it's a grungy place and it gets a grungy sound," he says. "That's just the way I like it—down and dirty." Forgetting about the ashtray, I toss a butt on the floor and stamp it out. "Hey, I can do that—you can't!" Ed says in mock-admonition, then laughs uproariously.

"C'mere, you little shit!" commands a familiar female voice, startling Van Halen. It's Valerie Bertinelli, all right, but she's not in the control room—we see and hear her on the surveillance video monitor, as she reprimands one of her cats. Ed looks relieved. A moment later, Mrs. Van Halen pokes her gorgeous head through the door to tell her hubby she's going to run some errands, and he assures her that he's hard at work—first the interview, then the session. She gives him a beatific smile and goes on her way.

According to bassist Mike Anthony, "It's weird, because Valerie comes back here periodically, and it never fails—every time she comes back here, we're in the other room either watching TV or playing video games."

What they're supposed to be doing is making a record. Since last October, the members of Van Halen Mach II and longtime engineer/co-producer Donn Landee have been coming up here to record what the principals consider a critical album in the life of this group. Even though *5150*—the first effort featuring replacement frontman Sammy Hagar—sold better than any previous VH album, the boys in the band attribute a lot of those sales to mere consumer curiosity. It isn't that they aren't proud of it—they regard the album as a big win by an underdog—but the members of VH II still feel like they've got something to prove. The new release, *OU812* (around here, they just call it "the rock and roll album"), is the first one to be undertaken with Hagar as the "throat" as well as Edward's lyricist/collaborator. (Ed, Al and Mike were already working up the material for *5150* when the Roth-to-Hagar transition took place.) It's also the first opportunity for this modified and newly inspired band to show what it can do as a road-tested unit. To hear the players talk, you'd think they were the Oakland Raiders of the John Madden era: a bunch of free spirits who broke all the rules and still won the Super Bowl—brash outlaws who regard victory (read: mega-sales) as the ultimate form of vindication (take that, Dave).

And, like the Raiders, they see themselves as macho guys with sensitive sides. On my follow-up visit to 5150, Hagar, a hippie to the core, spends a half-hour waxing poetic about the unfettered joys of Cabo San Lucas, the Baja resort town where he recently bought a condo. Hagar's already fantasizing about sitting *au naturel* on some secluded, rocky point in Baja, fishing and suckin' down the brewskis.

"I'm countin' the days, man," he assures me. "As soon as this is over, I'm outta here." Hagar was inspired to write a song lyric about his love affair with the place, and "Face Down in Cabo (Cabo Wabo)" is being mixed by Landee this very afternoon.

Al, Ed, Mike and several techies and roadies are sitting in the rec room watching *Dragnet: The Movie* on the big screen while they wait for Donn to complete a rough mix in the adjacent control room. After working out on *Captain Fantastic*, Sammy goes next door to see how "Cabo" is coming along.

The sentimental Anthony pulls me aside to tell me how excited he was after the first-take recording of *5150*'s "Summer Nights"—the moment everyone knew without a doubt that Hagar was their boy. "Donn played it back, and we were just all looking at each other— tears practically coming out of everybody's eyes. 'Whoa—this is gonna be something big! This is gonna happen!' It made the fur rise, you know?" he confides, holding up his forearm for my inspection.

Moments later, Hagar bursts into the room. "You gotta hear this, man—it's awesome!" he says to Eddie, who is seated on a couch. "Look!" the singer demands, holding his arm in front of Eddie's face and pointing at it, exactly as Anthony had done with me. "I showed Donn," Hagar continues, "and he said, 'Me, too!' " Apparently, the success of this album will be measured in terms of sales, airplay and erect body hair.

Suddenly, a monstrous sound erupts from the studio—Landee is playing back a rough mix, and he has cranked it up high enough to knock the squirrels from the trees. I hurry next door to get the full effect. Sitting at the console, the ordinarily pallid Landee has an aerobic flush in his cheeks as the monumental roar of "Cabo Wabo" shakes the building.

Van Halen stands in the doorway, motioning me toward him with a tilt of his head. He has to shout in my ear to make himself heard: "Donn doesn't want anyone else in the room when he's mixing." Oops. Feeling more like an interloper than an interviewer, I hustle out the door. During the track's breathtaking solo section, I watch Edward, his eyes flashing, pace the driveway with the feverish relentlessness of a leopard stalking its next victim. If the music is making his fur rise, he's not acknowledging it. I get the distinct feeling I'm not supposed to be hearing this yet—that Van Halen will serve no vinyl before its time. As the final note decays, he turns on his heels and walks back into the rec room.

During this brief sequence of events, I have a startling revelation: There are three Van Halens. The EVH who's known to the outside world is Eddie the rock star—the grinning dervish you see onstage and in pictures. Then there's Ed the good bud—a snickering, wisecracking everyman who exudes regular-guyness to his pals, who's no more ostentatious than a clump of dirt. But these two are subordinate to Edward the smoldering perfectionist—hermetic, protective, formidable. When push comes to shove in this band, enter Edward, a demanding leader with a killer instinct, accepting no less than optimum effort and absolute loyalty from his subordinates. Eddie mugs for the camera; Ed pokes his buddies in the ribs over dumb jokes in bad movies; Edward is a solipsistic wizard who coaxes supernatural sounds and rhythms from a piece of wood with six strings stretched across it.

Van Halen may come off as happy-go-lucky and just one of the guys, but behind his happy-face mask lie the cognitive/intuitive intricacies of an introspective artist who sets impossible goals for himself and unfailingly achieves them. Clearly, this man still has something to prove—not to the world, but to himself. More than virtuosity, it's his hair-raising ferocity of spirit that separates him from his imitators. The truth is, Edward Van Halen is the king of this hill—everything else is just jape.

So tell us, Ed—what makes Edward tick?

GUITAR WORLD I don't intend to dwell on the David Lee Roth issue— that's been done to death.

EDWARD VAN HALEN Good!

GW I'm primarily interested in understanding how you make your music. When you play in a trio, like you did for years...

VAN HALEN Like I'm still doing—a trio with a throat.

GW When you're playing with just a bass, guitar and drums, every element is crucial, but the guitarist carries most of the load.

VAN HALEN You gotta fill up the gaps. That's why I always used to use an Echoplex—it made a lot of noise, so it covered up a lot of shit! [*laughs*]

GW What you do—and what any really good guitarist does in a trio context—is play the spaces as much as the notes. And one of the things that's a hallmark of your style is the clipping of notes, which adds another level of rhythm. Sometimes it sounds fugue-like, almost—like a Bach harpsichord. You started on classical music, didn't you?

VAN HALEN Oh yeah, I was classically trained on piano up until I was 12.

GW But the first guitar you played was a flamenco guitar, right?

VAN HALEN Yeah, a nylon-string job.

GW There are a couple of things on your albums that demonstrate quite a bit of dexterity on the nylon-string; "Spanish Fly" is one of them. It's neat to hear that kind of attack on such a delicate-sounding instrument.

VAN HALEN It's sort of a funny thing how that happened. I think it was New Year's Eve back in '78 or '79. Alex and I were over at [*producer*] Ted Templeman's house, and there was this acoustic guitar sittin' in the corner. I started fooling around on it, y'know—I had half a beat going, and I said, "Mmmm, I feel like jamming a little bit." Ted walks in and he said, "Wow, you can play acoustic guitar?" I looked at him like, "What's the difference? It's got six strings—it's a guitar!" So I ended up coming up with "Spanish Fly."

GW Did you play a lot of acoustic guitar around the house?

VAN HALEN In the very, very beginning I did, because I couldn't afford an electric one.

GW Did you usually have an acoustic around, or did you just sort of go and become a lap player? You know what I mean by that?

VAN HALEN A lap player?

GW Yeah, you sit on your bed, you put the guitar on your lap and you play.

VAN HALEN Oh yeah! On the bed.

GW On the bed, in the motel room.

VAN HALEN Yeah, I did that for years, man.

GW So what was your first electric guitar?

VAN HALEN It was a Teisco Del Rey. Actually, I have a similar one upstairs.

GW Three pickups?

VAN HALEN Four pickups. It's funny, because now I use one.

GW You've been quoted as saying that you got your initial licks from Clapton, off the first Bluesbreakers album. Was that the case?

VAN HALEN Actually, I was totally into Cream, and then I started digging back and buying all the John Mayall stuff.

GW Your solo tone has always been really reminiscent of Clapton's—the tone he got by playing with his pick and then hitting the string with the top of his nail: doubling. I can see where the hammer-ons and all that evolved from that technique.

VAN HALEN I use my thumb and my middle finger when I pick. Actually, it depends. Normally, I pick like that, but when I do the hammer-on stuff I hold it this way [*wedges the pick between the first and second joints of his middle finger*]. A lot of people say, "Hey whaddaya do with your pick?"—because they don't see it. It's just right there. You see a lot of people stick the pick between their teeth, and I just had to figure out something else. And sometimes, when I use the wiggle stick, I hold it with my pinkie and pick like that [*holds the pick between his thumb and index finger, with the last three fingers slightly curled to form a fulcrum for the bar*], and pick the Mel Bay-style—the way you're supposed to, up and down, up and down. See, my bar is so loose that I don't have to keep these fingers straight.

As far as the hammer-on thing is concerned—I never really saw anybody do it, okay? I'm not saying, "Hey, I'm bitchin', I came up with it," but I never really saw anybody do it. But I got the idea a long time ago when I saw Led Zeppelin, back in '71 or something like that. Page was doing his guitar solo before "Heartbreaker," or in the middle of it [*hums guitar riff*]. He stood there playing [*hums some more*], and I think, Wait a minute, open string, pull off. I can do that. Use that finger up here, and use this as the nut, and move it around. That's how I first thought of it, and I don't know if anyone else did it. I just kind of took it and ran with it. People say, "Holy shit, man, you do it all over the place now, instead of just using open strings."

GW When did you integrate the technique into your style?

VAN HALEN Put it this way: since even before we started doing original tunes. I think I was actually doing that before I ever wrote a tune. I remember when we first started playing original sets, at the Whisky or Starwood, I'd turn around when I did it, because Al said, "Hey guys, be cool. Don't let those mothers rip you off!"

GW To return to playing in a three-piece context: Even when not playing strict rhythm—as you rarely do—good guitarists make the rhythmic stuff happen.

VAN HALEN I always felt that I was a rhythmic kind of player—I mean, in my leads. I have a weird sense of time. A lot of times I'll count something off, or I'll just start playing something, and Al will come in completely backward from the normal beat. It's almost a running joke in the band. I don't do it on purpose; I just kind of never come in on the "one."

> "It's kind of a magic that happens; **nothing is really calculated.**"

GW Your playing, on record, has an extreme blockbuster intensity that I suppose has to do, to a certain extent, with Donn Landee and his engineering. But how do you make it sound so "atomic bomb"?

VAN HALEN That's Donn, man, I don't know.

GW When you're working, you do a lot of first—and second—take solos.

VAN HALEN Oh, definitely. Nothing is really planned out. I don't know how to explain it, but when Donn gets here, talk to him for a minute. If you ask him, "How do you do what you do?" he'll say, "I don't know." I swear to God. Sometimes when Donn tries to think something out, it doesn't work. He'll just throw a couple of mikes out there and get a unique kind of thing happening. You can't learn it at Columbia School of Broadcasting—you know what I mean?

GW Is it that anything could work in a given situation—he has an idea, and you have an idea, they just come together and it works?

VAN HALEN It's kind of a magic that happens; nothing is really calculated.

GW That's one problem with trying to explain artistry: artists are the last ones who can explain it.

VAN HALEN Take my guitar sound—I don't think we've changed the way we mic. I've got a Shure 57 or 58 right up on the speaker; it's the only way I've ever miked my amp! We never try in a big room, a little room or far-miking or anything—just a mic right up.

GW I read recently about your Bradshaw rack, and thought, Where does he use it? Where is it?

VAN HALEN I really don't use it.

GW You got it because you can have one, but you don't use it. I hear DDL, a little phase, chorus, flanging—but it still sounds to me like a DiMarzio pickup or whatever it is pushing the Marshall amplifier. You get a lot of air.

VAN HALEN I go straight into my amp. When we're done here I'll show you what I use.

GW Have you recorded anything that mainly depended on an effect?

VAN HALEN Two things: MiniMoog on "Dancing in the Streets," because I didn't know what sequencers were or anything like that, so I just played the riff and added an echo; and "Cathedral," same thing—same record, as a matter of fact. I was in that echo mode. Those two things I couldn't do without the echo.

GW Would you say "Eruption" represents the crystallization of your approach to playing guitar? It's almost like a textbook study of your technique, and it's the number that led a million guitarists to think, Wow, I gotta figure out how he did that. And they still want to know. But maybe there isn't any secret to it.

VAN HALEN There ain't—not that I know of. What do you mean? What kind of secrets?

GW What do you think of Stanley Jordan?

VAN HALEN I respect him—I've seen him on the Johnny Carson show, seen him do his thing—but to me, what he's doing is eliminating other band members. He's taking tapping to the point where it's like more than one person playing; whereas I don't care to get into it that far. To me, it's just an extension of the way I play guitar—not, "Well, I want to play the bass, too." To me, that's so out there that it's like computerized shit, almost. Someone will hear it and go, "Wow, it sounds great," but it is so beyond that it's almost not special—I don't know how to explain it.

GW Does it have to do with the idea that when you play with a band— a drummer and a bass player—you're working off the energy of the other guys as well as your own?

VAN HALEN Oh yeah. There's a guessing game going on all the time, and there's the friction, a feeling of being on the edge of your seat— who's going to fall, who's gonna lose it first? It creates excitement. Whereas if you're doing it all yourself, it sounds like a guy with a drum machine and a sequencer, blowing a sax to it or something.

GW In a way, the rock band is like an endangered species now because of that technology. Kids who are learning how to play now have the sequencers and the computers and stuff, but they lack the interaction.

VAN HALEN That reckless abandon of falling down the stairs and hoping to land on your feet.

GW So you are doing God's work here, in a way, by inspiring people to fall down those stairs. To a certain extent, *5150* breaks with the pattern of your first six albums in the sense that, as you described in an earlier interview, you started tracks with keyboards, and also in that you take a more constructed approach.

VAN HALEN The reason being that that room isn't big enough for us to play drums and piano and mike 'em both at the same time! It wasn't on purpose. As soon as we're done with this record, I'm going to knock that back wall out and build another room to put the piano in. I was going crazy, telling Al, "Damn, I wish I could play

"I would love to have written a Christmas carol."

at the same time with you," but I couldn't, because miking the piano and miking the drums didn't work in the same room.

GW But why not overdub the keyboards?

VAN HALEN What's Al going to play to? The piano is the melody.

GW So what do you do, put a click down?

VAN HALEN No, uh-uh. No click, I just played the piano, MIDIed to my OB-8.

GW So you dictate the time with your innate sense of rhythm—and nothing else. Did you ever check it metronomically against real time?

VAN HALEN No, I just go by what feels right.

GW Is that the way you're working on this album as well?

VAN HALEN Yeah. This time around, there hasn't been a song yet where I play first and Al overdubs.

GW How's it working this time?

VAN HALEN Well, I haven't used the piano yet. I'm using synthesizers, but they're direct so there's no problem with bleed. There's one song where I overdubbed the piano. It's a pretty rocking album—there's no wimpy shit here. It's not necessarily back to basics, but it's rawer. We're actually out there playing live again. It's more a loose kind of trip. I remember that after we did *5150*, we said to each other, "Next record we're really going to put it together right." Instead it's the other way around!

GW Wasn't *5150* put together with less abandon?

VAN HALEN Only "Love Walks In" and "Dreams," because those were the piano tunes. They had to be thought out.

GW In terms of overall ambiance, "Why Can't This Be Love?" sounds like the most elaborate Van Halen song ever.

VAN HALEN It's because of the instrumentation. I used the arpeggiator in the OB-8, so everyone had to play to that. That's why it has kind of a uniform effect.

GW It sounds much more polished.

VAN HALEN It's more pop-popular, right? If more people like it, it's pop, right? What's wrong with that? I would love to have written a Christmas carol. What's wrong with that?

GW Do you ever feel limited by the specific demands of your audience? As in, "Maybe my public won't like it if there aren't at least three hammer-on solos."

VAN HALEN I don't think so. I'll do anything that I feel like doing. I have to like it. And if I like it, that's all that matters. I mean, it's kind of a stuck-up attitude maybe, but I really believe that I have to like it before I can even attempt to have anyone else like it.

GW What was your first serious guitar?

VAN HALEN I had a gold-top Les Paul with soap-bar pickups.

GW The thing about a Les Paul is, it always sounds like a Les Paul. No matter how much you try, you can't get it to sound like anything else. But when you play a Stratocaster-style guitar, you have to work at it harder.

VAN HALEN I never understood the difference—I can't tell. As a matter of fact, when I pick up a Paul now it's probably harder for me.

GW The Les Paul neck, to me, feels more like an acoustic guitar, whereas a Stratocaster...

VAN HALEN It was never this hand [*holds up his left hand*] that bothered me on any guitar; it was the other side, because the bridge on the Les Paul is higher, and I always rest the palm of my hand on the bridge—when I play a muffle, for example.

GW What about the gauge of the strings?

VAN HALEN I went through all kinds of phases. Just like with picks—I still don't know what I like. Sometimes I use fat ones, sometimes thin ones. String-wise, for a long time I used real heavy ones because I tuned way down to like D-flat, C♯.

GW You've even used a bass string.

VAN HALEN Oh yeah. That's kind of cool—an A and an A bass string.

GW And then that gets you into different tunings, too, I guess. So how do you figure that stuff out?

VAN HALEN I think the only tune I've ever really used a strange tuning on was "Top Jimmy" on *1984*. I just had this melody in my head and figured I'd just tune to the melody.

GW In that case, the melody just came into your head. Does it usually come to you that effortlessly?

VAN HALEN It takes me forever to write. I have to like something—I hate just puking something out. I could probably write you five tunes in the time we're here, but they'd be bullshit to me. You might like 'em, I don't know, but I have to like something. I don't please myself very easily, I guess. And it's not like a perfectionist kind of thing.

GW Do you know where they come from, the ideas? Do they just kind of pop into your head? Or do they pop into your fingers first?

VAN HALEN A lot of times, yeah. Sammy has this theory—his three-lock-box theory—where spiritually, mentally and physically, you gotta be together in order for anything creative to really happen. He had a song called "Three Lock Box," which a lot of people thought was about...[*runs his right index finger in and out of his left fist*] you know? It ain't—it's a pretty heavy thing. Actually, I agree with it. You can have an idea in your head, but if you can't execute it, what's the use? You got to have the technical shit down. That's what I mean when I say that it comes from your fingers sometimes. You'll be playing and, all of a sudden, you'll have an idea in your head and your fingers will just go with it. And the more you do that, and the more you listen to other things, something's bound to filter through and come out.

GW Do you practice a lot?

VAN HALEN It depends on what you call practicing. I never sat down and learned scales or said, "Oh wow, now I'm going to play a minor scale." What I do is, I just noodle; that's all I do—noodle.

GW You mean you just sit all the time with a guitar in your hands?

VAN HALEN Exactly. I just noodle.

GW So your attitude about what you really do, which is play the guitar—that's what you really do fundamentally, because everything else springs from that—hasn't really changed over the years.

VAN HALEN I guess. You can answer that better than me!

GW To many people, you're on that Hendrix level—you know, that ultimate rock guy level—and yet you're just the same regular guy you were all along. But there's so much stuff surrounding you—I'm sure many people want a piece of you. How do you deal with that?

Have you found a way to insulate yourself from all that attention and adoration?

VAN HALEN Maybe I don't deal with it, that's why I...

GW But you've managed to not be changed by it, which is the key.

VAN HALEN Well, I don't see how it can change someone, I really don't.

GW But you see where it does change people, though.

VAN HALEN Oh, I've seen people close to me change, you know? But I don't understand why. A lot of people, all they want is the fame. I'll take the fortune, you can have the fame. [*laughs*]

GW A fortune only allows you the freedom to do what you wanted to do in the first place. But if you become famous, you lose the freedom to do what you wanted to do.

VAN HALEN Exactly, it's catch-22, man—you're screwed no matter what you do. The one thing that keeps me kinda sane, though, is that I don't really know how to be pretentious.

GW Yeah, I can see that. Do you feel pressure from any particular sector at this point in your life? I'm sure Warner Bros. would like to have a record.

VAN HALEN There's no pressure, though I guess they do—I don't really think about it. I create my own pressure. I'm working on a tune right now, and I'm frustrated to death because I'm stuck. Everyone else says, "It sounds great—what are you worried about?" But something ain't jiving within my head, and I'm frustrated—it pisses me off.

GW What do you do when you get into a situation like that?

VAN HALEN I drink a couple of beers, smoke a couple of packs of cigarettes and try and walk away from it for a bit. Then I come back. I'm actually the type of person, though, who doesn't like to stay away. A lot of people think that if you're burnt on something, you should go on to something else and come back to it later. I can't do that. I believe that if you work through it, if you scale that wall, it'll be better than if you come back to it fresh and don't have the same frustrated attitude toward it. Because, when you come back, your attitude toward the song will be different—you're not fighting anymore.

GW So you use the frustration.

VAN HALEN In a funny way, I do. But I don't wish it upon anyone, because I don't like it.

GW But that's part of being an artist.

VAN HALEN Usually, when the frustration hits and I come through it, I have a better tune than something that came easy.

GW People have a tendency to rely too much on inspiration as opposed to getting down to it.

VAN HALEN I think the most frustrated I've probably ever been was with the intro to "Little Guitars," the little flamenco-like thing. This is a prime example of me overcoming this wall. I had this thing in my head, but had trouble with it because I can't fingerpick like that. I wanted to do [*sings guitar riff*].

GW That's called frailing.

"I'll take the fortune, **you can have the fame.**"

VAN HALEN Yeah, well whatever, I can't do that. I said, "I gotta put this on a record, because I've got this melody and I wanna do it." So I just took an open E, fanned the thing and did the pull-offs on the low E. Let me show you. [*continues talking while strapping on his 5150 guitar.*] Where there's a will, there's a way, whether you call it cheating or not. The end result is how it sounds, right? [*starts flamenco noodling on guitar.*] I forget exactly how it went. But I remember when we were mastering the record over at Amigo, Warner Bros. Studios, Steve Lukather and the guys were there, listening, and they said, "Wow, I didn't know you could play like that." I said, "I don't." [*laughs*]

GW I notice that you have the action on this a little higher than on your other guitars, and the strings are a lighter gauge.

VAN HALEN That's not on purpose—it's mostly because I didn't put it together right. I use .009, .011, .016, whatever—regular slinkies. I'm not real good at setting up guitars.

GW Look, it's got cigarette burns on it. This is a rock guitar, man.

VAN HALEN [*snickering*] The backside's real nice, too.

GW You've finally got everything the way you want—you've pretty much solved all the problems you had in the past.

VAN HALEN Don't get me wrong—I don't think our first six albums were bad or anything. I think we did some good stuff. It's just different now, different chemistry happening—a different quarterback, so to speak, or we're running different plays. We won the Super Bowl last year. And we're gonna be the first ones to do it twice in a row. In my mind, I go by how I feel about what we do, whether we even release it or not. I dig what we're doing, the new stuff...it's inspiring to me. If I write something and when I play it back, my fur rises, that's like, "Whoa, where did that come from?" It's spooky. When I hear something that I did, and I'm not really conscious of the fact that that's me, that blows me away, always. I love that! There are a lot of moments like that on this record.

GW Can you cite specific moments on past records where you had that feeling?

VAN HALEN Not right off the bat. There were some solos I did on *Fair Warning* that kind of gave me the chills. That was our worst-selling album to date, the fourth one. It was kind of a dark album—it was a bad time in my life. There's a lot of interesting guitar on it, though.

GW So you were pulling on the downside of your emotions.

VAN HALEN You know, you go with what you've got. I wasn't consciously trying to be down. [*laughs*]

GW The solos are great on that record.

VAN HALEN It's weird stuff.

GW Earlier you referred to a problem you've been having with one song.

VAN HALEN Well, it's only been a problem since yesterday—I just came up with it yesterday, and I'm stuck.

GW Is that just a song, or is it something that's going to be on this album?

VAN HALEN I'd like it to be on the record.

GW So this album isn't completely nailed down yet.

VAN HALEN Yeah, I'd say we're about two-thirds of the way into it. We've got nine tracks, and I always like to have a couple extra. I like to drop the needle at the beginning and listen all the way through, and if something isn't right, I like to be able to say, "Well, maybe this song would make it flow well."

GW Do you ever say to yourself, "Well, we could use another one of these kind of songs?"

VAN HALEN No-no-no, I can't do that, because I can't write on demand. I guess some people can. They say, "We need a song like this," and they'll contrive a tune similar to what they think they need. But I can't do that. I don't know how other people write, or where their inspiration or ideas come from. But me, I just have to go with what comes out, which makes it tough sometimes. Sometimes nothing comes out; other times what does come out comes in little spurts, and if I don't go with it right then... Sometimes I'll think,

Aaaah, I'll work on it some more tomorrow, and I'll totally forget what track I was on.

GW When you first come up with an idea, do you just put it on cassette?

VAN HALEN Sometimes I'll hum it into a little microcassette. I remember once a few years ago, when we toured down in South America, Valerie was sleeping and I didn't want to wake her up, so I went in the closet. [*laughs*] What it ended up being was "Girl Gone Bad" on *1984*. Oh man, it'd be funny if I could play you the tape, but I don't know where it is.

GW There must be a certain point where you say, "Okay, I can anticipate the recording of another album, so I've got to get some songs together." Do you try to sort of schedule a time where you write the bulk of the songs, and then...

VAN HALEN No. See, for one, I don't consider this my career—it's my life. It's not like I go to work, and now I'm going to map out when I'm going to work and stop working. It's just kind of a continuous, round-the-clock thing—whenever it hits, I do it. It's been almost two years since the last record, partly because I just wanted to spend time with the family. Also, I did Sammy's record, and we definitely didn't want a Van Halen record out there at the same time as his. People were saying, "Huh? Is he in Van Halen or what? Who's gonna be the next singer?" No, it's just kind of an ongoing thing. I don't say, "Okay, now I'm gonna write, and stockpile some tunes, so when we record I'll be ready." Actually, I walked in pretty cold this time. I said, "Well, do you want to start?" "Okay, whaddaya got?" "Call me tomorrow!"

GW But you did get to a point where the ideas were popping out, because you were psyched up.

VAN HALEN Oh, yeah. I guess when I put my mind in that mode, when the electricity starts happening, it just kind of happens.

GW Was there a particular song idea that generated a lot of your momentum? The first one that really made sense to you?

"I don't consider this my career —it's my life."

VAN HALEN Yeah, the one I was just starting to play.

GW The one that started with the keyboard?

VAN HALEN It's kind of an inspired tune, and it really started the ball rolling.

GW What's that going to be called?

VAN HALEN "When It's Love" or "How Do You Know When It's Love?"

GW There seems to be an element of consistency in the way you approach things. Do you feel like you're a better musician now than you were eight or nine years ago?

VAN HALEN I don't know. Sometimes I hear an old tune on the radio, and I think, How did I do that? Whereas, if it was back then and I were to hear what I'm doing now, I'd probably say the same thing. So I don't know. I think I'm better at executing my ideas.

GW Do you feel you've reached a certain plateau?

VAN HALEN Yeah, in a funny way. I used to hit plateaus all the time when it came to riffs, soloing, because I got sick of hanging in the same area with the guitar, trying to squeeze the most out of those same notes. I guess playing keyboards has helped a lot, because now I have another instrument to bozo out on.

GW So that'll keep you from ultimately getting burned out on the guitar, since you can always go to another instrument. But you're still in the same mindset.

VAN HALEN Right. I want to learn how to play sax, too. Oh, I love sax. Guitar is actually kind of like sax—like some of the old Cream guitar tones. Allan Holdsworth, he sounds like he's blowin'!

GW Have you tried a guitar synthesizer?

VAN HALEN Everyone asks me that. No! I tried one years ago, and it didn't track for shit. And to me, it's like you have to alter your playing for this sound. At least that's what I remember. This was, like, five years ago, when Roland developed them. You can't just plug into it. For one thing, you've gotta play their guitar, you know—I think there's one company that had the thing that slides underneath your pickup—but you can't just play normal guitar and then layer that on top of it. You have to adapt to it, and I don't like that. And besides, I play keyboards; so if I want any kind of fancy shit, I'll just do it with 10 fingers. I don't think the guitar synthesizers have really found a spot on this planet.

GW You don't need it, basically.

VAN HALEN No, I don't. That's the bottom-line reason I'm not interested. If I want electronic stuff I'll play it on keyboards. Why bastardize the guitar?

GW How do you know when an idea's gonna relate more to keyboards than to the guitar, and vice versa?

VAN HALEN When I get an idea in my head, it's either on keyboard or guitar. I guess I come up with different stuff on guitar than on keyboard. But then in the old days I'd come up with riffs, like on "And the Cradle Will Rock..." that I played on a Wurlitzer electric piano through my Marshalls, and that was kind of like a guitar riff that I put to keyboard. "Hear About It Later" from *Fair Warning* was actually a piano riff that I put to guitar. I don't know if I'm answering your question, but...

GW It's just whatever's closer at hand?

VAN HALEN I have no set approach, because often I'll be sitting around humming a riff and envisioning that on the piano, and other times I'll be humming and I'll be thinking guitar.

GW It does sound like you're getting a little more systematic about how you approach things.

VAN HALEN Obviously, once we start a record, there's a schedule. And sometimes we don't meet schedules! [*laughs*] It's like right now, our manager's asking, "When's it gonna be done?" I say, "Damned if I know! When it's done, I'll let you know." I can't do it like that, otherwise I'll puke it out. But then again, I'm not the type of person who really likes to sit there and brew on the stuff for too long either. If I lose interest, forget it.

GW A song is a series of guitar licks as much as it is verses, choruses and a bridge, right? It all just kind of comes out in this one block of...

VAN HALEN Well, sometimes it doesn't. Sometimes I'll have just one riff, and then I'll say, "Where do I go from here?"

GW Now that you've got things set up pretty much the way you want, do you ever think about doing an instrumental album? Or are you getting all the creative satisfaction you need?

VAN HALEN I think I get my rocks off pretty well. I don't have any deep, hidden things that I want to get out. I do what I do, and everything seems to fit. If I wanna do a long solo, I'll do a long solo—no one's telling me I can't. A lot of the tunes on this record are long, too—so far there's no song under five and a half minutes—and three or four of them are over seven minutes. We'll have to cut them down a little bit. I don't know how we're gonna do that, either.

GW You guys are usually pretty concise. Even those little intros, and the little connectors between cuts, are like complete ideas in themselves. Do you have anything like that happening on this album?

VAN HALEN Yeah, there are a couple of little things like that on this one. I don't know, I always like to kinda have something to start off a tune, to set the mood for it.

GW It can be the intro to the song.

VAN HALEN They're sort of like little commercials between songs, know what I mean? Like, "Hey, buy Tide, Super-Improved Tide," and then the next song starts. Now that I think about it, the intros that I've done—guitar things like "Cathedral" or "Little Guitars"—really have nothing to do with the song before or after.

GW How do you warm up?

VAN HALEN I just pick up the guitar and noodle. Most of the time, what I'm trying to do is write a new tune. I think more in terms of songs than I do riffs. Just doing licks. In the old days, when I first started learning how to play lead, all I'd do is try and figure out little leads. Once you get to the point where you can pretty much execute anything that pops into your head, you start thinking more song, I guess. At least I do. So when I warm up, I just kind of noodle and hum shit in my head. I write probably 90 percent of my tunes on tour— either during soundcheck or warming up for the gig.

GW That's interesting. I recently spoke with the guys in Squeeze, who told me that in order to write, they had to be at home where they follow a self-imposed regimen.

VAN HALEN Well, to actually put things down on tape, yeah. But on tour, I'll have the seeds of a hundred songs, and come home and listen to little bitty ideas of things.

GW On a microcassette?

VAN HALEN Actually, I've only used the microcassette machine a few times. Usually I remember the idea. But at the same time, out at the beach I got a piano, and a couple of guitars, and if something pops in my head I'll just pick up the guitar and jam, or play piano.

GW You think pretty much in the standard mode of music, right? You don't deal with weird modalities or...

VAN HALEN I don't think in terms of scales at all. I just think whatever pops into my head. Like sometimes I do some weird intervals or chord changes, and I hate it when people say "Hey, he just went from a this to a that." So fuckin' what?

GW I've heard lead guitar described as pattern playing and scale playing.

VAN HALEN That sounds the same to me. I'm just kind of a "wing it" player.

GW You're working on a record, and that presupposes dealing with deadline pressure—no matter where you record. But you have your own studio—you can set up a casual schedule, if you want. Do you have to discipline yourself to avoid being overly casual?

VAN HALEN Here's the thing: Every day we say, "Okay, we'll start at 2:00 tomorrow." And then I'll stay overnight here, or be here by noon, messing around. Sammy shows up at 2:30, Donn gets here at maybe 1:30. Then Mike will get here at 3:00 and go in there and play pinball or goof off until about 4:00. And then we'll leave at 5:30. The next day, Mike'll say, "My car broke down—I gotta take it to the shop. I'll be a little late." And we'll say, "Why don't we just blow it off today?" We actually started recording, I think, in October, one day a month. [*laughs*] Nahh, that's an exaggeration—it was maybe two days a week for a couple hours. One good thing about having Ted around—he really cracked the whip.

GW But when you get down to it, you must get a lot accomplished if you're able to be that casual about it, yet still wind up with the record you want.

VAN HALEN Chris [*Pollan*], our tour manager, always says, "You guys, man, you watch television, play a song once, come back, watch television for another hour, play a song once, man...what kinda life is this?" [*laughs*] Because really, in a day, we probably get maybe 45 minutes of work out, and we're here maybe from 2 P.M. to 7 P.M.

GW So they're not marathon sessions at all. You never do a real long one?

VAN HALEN Well, it varies. If we're onto something, we'll take it until we're down.

GW Earlier, you said that you've come to think more in terms of writing rather than playing. When an idea for a song strikes you, what comes first, the melody or the changes? Or does that vary?

VAN HALEN Usually the melody. Most of the riffs that I come up with, or pieces of music, are melodic little ditties. They're things that I hum in my head and play.

GW At what stage of development does a musical idea have to be in before you show it to Sammy?

VAN HALEN I'll have an intro, a verse, a B-section, a chorus and a solo section. I'll pretty much have the parts for a completed song.

GW Do you put it on tape for him? Do you get it to the stage where you say, "Okay, now it's ready"?

VAN HALEN No. We cut the tracks when we're all here.

GW What I mean is, do you put the guitar parts on a cassette?

VAN HALEN Yeah, I'll either do that or play it for him live. Al and I will play it, with the beat, and then Sammy'll say, "Go here from that point, instead of where you went." I'll try it, and if it works we'll do it. If not...You know, it's a band thing. Whenever you've got four people together, one's bound to not like everything you do. I come up with the parts, though, and we'll either all piece it together or I'll do it myself. It's not really set which way.

GW Does Sammy ever come in with a lyric and turn the tables?

VAN HALEN You mean inspire me to write music to the lyric? Not yet.

GW So far, you've cut eight tracks for the record. Will there be any more?

VAN HALEN A couple more, yeah. This one today, I hope.

GW You mean, you just had this idea on Thursday, and on Monday it's going to be recorded?

VAN HALEN Yeah. Why wait? When things happen, they happen fast. Sammy's got a place down in Cabo, Mexico. He wrote a song called "Cabo Wabo," about being smashed, you know. Anyway, that was done, like, in two days. I came up with it one day; next day we cut it. It came together real quick. Actually, though, I don't really write here. I don't write in the studio. I'll get the ideas either in the house, or at the beach, or wherever I am. Here is where I put it together. I never really come up with the seeds of songs here.

GW You've got all these electronic distractions here. I guess just being with your guitar and being...

VAN HALEN That's not necessarily it. I just look at the studio as a place where you put it all together, where you make it a real thing.

GW Is there a particular place where ideas have often come to you over the years?

VAN HALEN In bed, right before I fall asleep, I come up with all kinds of shit. Right as I start to drift off.

GW When you wake up it's still there?

VAN HALEN Well, not always.

GW Have you cut any of the solos to the new record yet, or are you waiting?

VAN HALEN I've done a few, yeah. A lot of 'em are live.

GW So you're following your usual procedure.

VAN HALEN Right. Usually, if it's an uptempo kind of rocker, I just blaze through it; whereas if it's a real melodic kind of tune, I like to think out a melodic solo. I'll play a rhythm track and then overdub the solo.

GW Do you ever splice your solos together?

VAN HALEN Oh, we've done compilations, sure. Sometimes I'll do three solos, and I'll say, "I like the beginning of that one, I like the end of that one, and I like the middle of that one." Whatever sounds good—there are no rules. And I ain't proud; I don't give a damn if I get it in one take or not! If it gets me off, it's fine.

GW Whenever I've seen pictures of you playing, in videos or whatever, you always have a big smile on your face. Is that for the camera, or...?

VAN HALEN No, I'm just having a good time! I'm just a happy guy, I guess. It's funny, because usually, whenever there's a camera in front of my face, I shy away from it. I'm not that kind of guy, you know? I'm not a camera flirt. I'm just kinda grooving, having fun. I'm laughing at something or somebody, or something I did that I got away with. My attitude's always been, "If you can't get out there in your boxer shorts and your ax, you're screwed!"

I ARRIVE AT THE STUDIO at the agreed-upon time, and Van Halen strides up to my car, probably wondering what I'm doing there. When I explain that Landee has offered me a chance to discuss the completed album, he tells me that only seven of the 10 cuts have been mixed, and that Landee hasn't arrived yet. While I content myself with shooting baskets, the master of the estate ambles back and forth between the clubhouse and Valerie Villa. Ed must be getting in shape for the Monsters of Rock tour—he's now drinking Koala coolers instead of Heineken, and he's smoking Merit Ultra Lights instead of Marlboros (although there are boxes of the latter sitting on various surfaces in the rec room).

When Landee still hasn't arrived by 1 P.M., I start to banter with Ed, hoping to steer the conversation around to the new album. But that isn't necessary—he brings up the subject himself, ebulliently explaining that this is the first album he's made that he can't stop listening to. "It still makes my fur rise," he tells me.

"I'm just a happy guy, I guess."

We head into the control room and take a look at the song list, which Landee has written out on a sheet of legal pad. There's a big surprise at the bottom of the page: Van Halen has covered Little Feat's "Apolitical Blues," the original version of which Landee recorded 16 years earlier with Ted Templeman. The tune is slated for the CD and cassette versions of *OU812*, as well as for the B-side of the first single, fronted by "Black & Blue," a heavy, mid-tempo rocker that Ed considers to be the most characteristically Van Halen track on the album.

The album is scheduled to be mastered this Friday, and Ed and Valerie are embarking on their seventh-anniversary vacation on the following Tuesday. Nevertheless, Van Halen is still hedging on the album title. "I just wanna call it *Rock and Roll*," he says, "because that's what it is. It ain't heavy metal, it's not hard rock—it's rock and roll."

So what about the tunes, Ed?

"Now wait a minute," he cautions me, as I began jotting down the song titles on the list. "I wouldn't write the titles down yet. This first one, 'Naturally Wired,' we might call that 'AFU,' because the chorus is 'I'm all fired up.' Then again, the rideout is 'I'm naturally wired.' So it's either 'Naturally Wired,' 'All Fired Up' or 'AFU.' 'Finish What You Started' could be 'Baby Come On' or 'Come on Baby.' And 'Source' or 'Source of Infection'..."

Is that an AIDS song?

"No-no-no. I first wanted to call the album that. You know, Van Halen *Source of Infection*—'music that's infectious.' Actually, Sammy came up with it, and I saw it that way. Al grossed out. He said, 'Sounds like a sore or somethin'.' I went, 'Okay, screw it.' I mean, we got a list like that of album titles. I don't know why they put *OU812* in that press release. Probably [*VH manager*] Ed Leffler just thought, since that was the latest one we bounced off of him, that's the one we decided on. *Rock and Roll*—I think that's classic. To me, though, an album title or a song title does not sell anything. It's just to let people know you got a new one out. Like Chicago—1-2-3-4-13-15-18... 'Hey—we got a new one.' Who gives a damn what it's called? Call it *Mustard* on *Your Leg* or something—here's the new one. Call it *Yogurt!*"

I learn that the tune that gave Van Halen difficulties during my first visit to 5150 has become "Feels So Good," which Ed describes as a keyboard-powered pop song. (As I later discover, it's one of this album's most delightful surprises.)

"Yeah, I was kinda stumped on it, but I got past the hump. That one and 'When It's Love' are the most overdubbed songs. 'Apolitical Blues' is totally live except for the piano overdub that I did. It's just a sloppy blues. I tried to play it like [*Little Feat pianist*] Billy Payne. I'm not really that kind of player, but it was tripped-out, man, trying to do these slippery blues licks on piano and land on your feet. We spent like half an hour on it; Donn just hung two overhead mikes and that was it. It's so gross-sounding. I played slide on that black Airline guitar, through a little Music Man amp, and got a sound that's almost identical to the one Lowell [*George*] got. It's naaasty."

Ed runs down the song list with his blue Fender medium guitar pick. "I laid direct on 'Baby Come On,' 'Finish What You Started' or 'Come on Baby,' he says with a snicker. "Al was alone in there," he adds, pointing to the room on the other side of the glass, "so the drums sound real cool. Sammy and I were in here direct [*with Hagar strumming an acoustic*], and Mike was in here, too, playing. So the three of us are standing here waving, saying, 'Hey Al, having fun out there?'

"Then there's 'Cabo'—that's either 'Face Down in Cabo' or 'Cabo Wabo.' That one we recorded in a real weird way—the room just for the drums, Mike's bass direct, and I put my amp in the middle room," he says, referring to the tape storage area between the control room and the rec room. "I didn't know where else to put it—I didn't want to overdub to the bass and drums; I wanted to play live. So I stood in here, me and Mike played together, and my amp was in there. It's funny, because Valerie and everybody were in the rec room watching TV, and they couldn't hear anything but the guitar.

"I used a Fender 12-string on 'Cabo'—except for the solo, of course. There's a wah-wah on the solo—barely audible, though. I just used it for the sustain, not like Clapton wah-wah. I used the Bradshaw on 'Black & Blue.' I don't remember where else. I don't like a lot of jape—just a little bit of tasty echo to fill it out a little bit, sometimes a little Harmonizer. I mean, what else do you really need? What other effects are there? I'm not into effects, so I don't really even know what's out there. See, like all this stuff here," he says, pointing toward the built-in console, "is basically just different kinds of echoes and different kinds of doublings—that's it. I don't want no room simulator for my guitar! I got rooms."

Let's get back to *OU812*—or whatever the album will ultimately be called.

"This is the most unusual album we've done in terms of the way it was done," Ed says. "We wrote one song, put it down, wrote another one, put it down—we concentrated on one song at a time. Whereas with every other record, we'd put down all the basic tracks and then overdub. The first one I wrote was 'When It's Love.' I was so focused into that song that it took me a couple of days to think about another tune. Second one was 'Mine All Mine'—since I figured, Might as well get two keyboard tunes out of the way. When I was writing that, I had to change gears, because 'When It's Love' was still in my head, and it took me a bit to shift. And then, I was so into 'Mine All Mine' that I totally forgot how to play 'When It's Love.' Understand what I'm saying? And that went on with every song, because we didn't do them all in a row. The only two that I had seeds of ideas for when we started were 'Naturally Wired' and 'Black & Blue.' Everything else was written as we went along—and basically I wrote pretty quickly. Like 'Cabo'—I wrote that in one day."

Did Sammy bring in any lyrics for Ed to write music to?

"No, he would get inspired by the music. Actually, Sammy wanted to write a song about Cabo. He had just come back from there and I had just written the music. And he said, 'This is perfect for Cabo!'

"You know," Ed reflects, "I haven't heard a rock and roll record like this in a long time. Maybe I'm just out of touch or something, but there's so many different things on it. I dunno. I guess I'm just real happy with it. I'm jazzed."

What are his choices for singles?

"To me, 'When It's Love' is just a classic tune," Ed replies, going down the list again. "It's pretty, it's heavy, it's melodic, it's singalong... it's just a happening song. Whereas 'Black & Blue' is heavy funk—it's slippery, it's grungy, more of a kids'...what am I talkin' about—I'm a kid. But I'd like the first single to be something grungier. I don't want people to think, Oh, Van Halen went pop.

"There's only two songs on here that are keyboard-oriented. What I'm sayin' is, 'When It's Love' and 'Feels So Good' are very melodic songs, which people could consider pop and not Van Halen. Whereas 'Mine All Mine' is a keyboard tune, but it's smokin'. I doubled the keys with the guitar, and it sounds tripped-out. And 'Finish What You Started' will totally trip people out—it sounds like a cross between the Stones and us. It's probably the most atypical thing you'll ever hear from us—outside of 'Apolitical Blues.' When the Scorpions came up here, first thing we played them was 'Finish What You Started,' just to freak them out. They were sitting here going, 'Oh ja, ja. Ees very nice...' But they were looking at each other like, 'Was that them?' And then my brother walked in and said, 'Hey, you guys are doing a great job pretending you like it.' " Ed breaks up with laughter at the recollection.

"I'll play anybody anything from this record," he says, "Because everything's such a different vibe. You hear 'Apolitical Blues' and you say, 'That's Van Halen?!' I go, 'Yeah—hey, man, there's more than one side to Van Halen.' "

Maybe even the critics will go for this one.

"Oh, fuck the critics. You can print that. It's nice if they like them; it's also nice if they don't. Because they don't buy them anyway—they get them for free."

Tell us about the rest of the tunes.

" 'Sucker' (or 'Sucker in a three-piece') is kind of like a 'Panama' beat. 'Source' is a major fast boogie—really cookin'. It's got a neat intro, too. Oh, you know what's got a real weird intro is 'Naturally Wired,' or whatever we're calling that one. It's hard to figure out where the beat is, because Al doesn't start out on the 'one.' It's actually a drum beat I came up with years ago, and Al said, 'Hey, man—this beat would be great for this one.' I don't know, it's probably something Zeppelin would have done. And then I come in with finger-tappin' stuff, and you can't figure out what's going on until we all come in, and you say, 'Oh, there's the beat.' Hey, and here's Donn!"

Landee walks into the control room, just two hours behind schedule—which is precisely in keeping with the way this album was made. "Hey, Donn, why don't you play some of the stuff for him?" I've just hit pay-dirt. Van Halen exits, and Landee racks up a tape of completed mixes, cranks the master volume to 11, and lets 'er rip. In these circumstances, through the huge monitors, the music is nothing less than astounding, especially "When It's Love," a rock anthem if ever there was one; "Cabo," a slithering mass of interlocked riffs and rhythms; "Finish What You Started," wherein Edward's fingerpicked direct Strat picks up where "Honky Tonk Women" left off; and "Feels So Good," an exhilarating marriage of buoyant keyboards and breakneck drumming. Alex is a monster throughout the album (Ed explained that his brother stopped drinking, which made a huge difference in his drum work), and Edward is nothing less than spectacular at simply being Edward. Wow.

As Landee plays the cuts, my tape recorder continues to roll—most likely overloading from the volume. When Ed returns and sees my machine recording, he instantly metamorphoses into Edward. "Hey, what's this?" he demands. Oops. "I'm making a bootleg," I deadpan. "Actually, I forgot to turn it off." Edward isn't buying it, but Ed reappears before things get gnarly. "Hey, you'll get your free CD soon enough," he jokes, before rewinding my tape to the top of the music and ensuring that the tunes will be overlayed by talk. Fair enough, Ed.

We get back into a listening mode, and Van Halen pushes my chair into the middle of the room so I'll get the full effect. He seems quite eager to get an honest reaction from the first outsider to hear this music. He repeatedly leans over and yells comments in my ear. During "When It's Love," he shouts, "Check this out—this solo is really different"; and, in the middle of the solo section: "Clapton. See, I still have some of that in me." While "Feels So Good" plays, he says, "Makes me want to dance—and I don't dance!" and launches into an impromptu Van Halen hip-hop.

You know something? This is fun. As a matter of fact, I'm beginning to notice a tingling sensation spreading over my entire body. Whaddaya know—this stuff is making my fur rise. I present my forearm to Ed for inspection.

"See?!" Ed/Eddie/Edward shouts triumphantly over the glorious sounds of a great band at its absolute zenith. "The chill factor. That's what rock and roll is all about—it's a feeling."

REPRINTED FROM *GUITAR WORLD*, FEBRUARY 1990

[10]

"If I wanna play keyboards or if I wanna play tuba,
I'll play it."
—*EDDIE VAN HALEN*

THE MONSTER
OF ROCK

He sparked an Eruption—and an aftershock of
monumental proportions: Edward Van Halen,
Guitar World's player of the decade.

BY JOE BOSSO

"**L**OOK AT THIS MESS!**"** Eddie Van Halen takes in the barren and dusty confines of the apparent wreck and ruin of 5150, his beloved recording studio/clubhouse. Where most men find rest and rumination in neighborhood bars, Eddie has for years sought refuge in this, his hangout-joint to end all hangout-joints. Here he stays up late, pours back some Buds with his buds, and plays his videos. Here, too, he cranks it to hell and back, capturing bits of genius on two-inch tape.

But at this moment he couldn't nail a solo banjo track in here, let alone the monstrous sonic booms for which Van Halen is universally celebrated. 5150 is being remodeled, so everything's been stripped away, sawed-off, gutted. Amps, effects racks, consoles—all gone.

Construction will take at least a few months to complete, at which time the dream-like studio will sport a new look and house, for the first time, a drum room. But on this picture-perfect Hollywood day, poor Eddie Van Halen looks like a man without a country.

"What are you gonna do?" he shrugs, accompanying *Guitar World* Associate Publisher Greg Di Benedetto and I out onto the driveway. "That's where we're building the new house." He motions across the small valley that lies between the Van Halens' modest (by rock star and TV actress standards) one-bedroom digs and their soon-to-be constructed palatial estate. Half-a-dozen workmen are engaged in various digging, pouring and pounding activities. The house glistens in the L.A. sun and, while unfinished, looks like an architect's dream. Eddie grins a grin as only he can, lights a cigarette and assesses the situation with characteristic amusement. "The thing's taking twice as long as it was supposed to, and it's costing six times as much!"

EVH looks good: California-tanned, thinner than he's been in recent years and sturdy. He pads about the room, casually comfortable in beyond-baggy jeans, T-shirt and well-worn sneakers, with the cool, somewhat oblivious air peculiar to the mega-rich. For all that, it almost seems as if Eddie Van Halen is really just another guy, a bud—a dude. Perhaps that's how he likes it—as if the Porsches, Mercedes and Lamborghinis cluttering the driveway and parking lot could disappear tomorrow and it really wouldn't be that big a deal. Most successful rockers would take a journalist down to the wine cellar, but Eddie's idea of fun is showing off his motorized skateboard ("You can really clock yourself on the head when you fall off that thing at 35!"), or visiting his guitar room for a little stroll down memory lane.

"This place is a bit of a mess, too," he explains, running his hands along the bodies of guitar after guitar, as if to reacquaint himself with his collection of lovelies. "I don't usually keep 'em in cases because guitars are meant to be functional, you know?" [Later in the day, as we prepared to drive into downtown L.A. for a photo shoot, Eddie took his famous Frankenstein striped Strat and his 5150 guitars, among others, and tossed the whole bunch in the back of his pickup truck like they were two-by-fours. As each guitar landed with a loud thud, I gave Eddie a somewhat astonished, quizzical look. He simply grinned. "I don't use cases for these either!"]

"There's the Electro-Harmonix over there," he points to the keyboard just near the stairs. "I used that on 'Sunday Afternoon in the Park.' And there's the Destroyer I used to use," he says, pointing to one of the guitars hanging on the wall. "That was the one on *Women and Children First*. Oh, and here's what a Variac looks like!" Eddie's enthusiasm waxes as he holds up a harmless-looking electrical device that is most commonly used to dim wall lights. Eddie, of course, has for years routinely slapped them in his amps to better modify the voltage.

He ambles back outside where, plopped on a picnic table near the swimming pool, he reflects on a career that has not only brought him worldwide acclaim, fame and untold wealth, but, more importantly, has forever changed the way people play and listen to the electric guitar.

Although it is difficult today to imagine modern rock guitar without Eddie's influence, surprisingly, when the group that bears his surname released their debut album in early 1978, they were perceived as something of a throwback. While most popsters were caught up in the minimalism of post-punk, with its arty blend of end-of-the-world nihilism and Euro-style detachment, along came this louder-than-loud Southern California band of party-crazed Gypsies, blowing up amps and pillaging any unsuspecting town in their path. Their equipment was crude and their songs were empty-headed supplications to the pleasures of limitless wine, women and song. At a time when Gary Numan and Kraftwerk were setting the trends and the electric guitar was taking a backseat to the synthesizer, it appeared that this band didn't stand a chance.

Enter the round-cheeked Eddie Van Halen. As fast as he could unleash a flurry of dizzying harmonics, he tapped his way into our hearts, the first to infuse the electric guitar with genuinely new blood since Jimi Hendrix. For even if the young Van Halen's recording career had ended the moment he unplugged after tracking the seminal solo *tour de force* "Eruption," his place in the history of the electric guitar would have been assured. With this much-imitated instrumental, Van Halen single-handedly introduced the hammer-on to a generation of guitarists. Not only did "Eruption" serve to usher in an important, unconventional artist, it signaled the rise of something greater than that—it launched a movement. Overnight, the stakes were forever altered—and guitarists worldwide knew it seconds after their needles hit Van Halen vinyl.

In 1982 Eddie, by then an established rock star (a term he despises), received a call from producer Quincy Jones, who was working on a red-hot rock and roll track for a Michael Jackson album. Would Eddie come to the studio and lay down a solo? Sure, thought Eddie, why not? Might be fun. David Lee Roth had always frowned upon the idea of Eddie playing on other people's records, but hey, this was a Michael Jackson record, so Van Halen fans certainly wouldn't be interested—probably wouldn't even hear it. Eddie grabbed his guitar and split for the studio. Once there, he found that he liked what he heard, the driving song called "Beat It." The track was pretty much all there; Steve Lukather had recorded most of the guitars, and all that was needed was a solo—a hot one, to really make the tune cook.

After making the crucial suggestion that he solo over the verse section rather than the breakdown, as was originally planned, Eddie winged it. The solo would turn out to be Eddie's most popular and most analyzed work of the Eighties. All fired up, whooping and swirling, growling and shrieking, it is the product of a heart meeting a mind and connecting with the unknown.

It's a head-turner, all right, and for more than the obvious reasons. Eddie Van Halen was the perfect choice to play the solo, and his cameo spot on a Michael Jackson song carried repercussions that went far beyond guitar heroics. Until then MTV, still in its infancy, had maintained an unwritten rule against the airing of "black"-oriented videos. Although the network somewhat reluctantly agreed to air Jackson's "Billie Jean," it was a hollow victory, a response borne more out of record company pressure than popular opinion. But Eddie's star-turn on "Beat It" demolished the color barrier with stunning, decisive force. MTV had to respond. And it didn't end there. Suddenly, FM hard rock stations, which primarily catered to white suburbanites, were deluged with calls for "Beat It." Across the country, white males, who ordinarily would never dream of buying a Michael Jackson album, were doing so in record numbers. At the same time, black stations—the last places one would expect to hear searing, burning, heavy metal guitar—were wearing out their copies of "Beat It."

It seemed appropriate that Van Halen's brilliant and influential solo was the product of a whim. For this artist is—musically and personally—the personification of explosive spontaneity.

Eddie sits back in his chair, lights another cigarette, and grins that grin. The greatest guitarist in the world is ready to talk about 10 incredible years gone by.

GUITAR WORLD What is the single thing you're most proud of having accomplished in the last decade?

EDDIE VAN HALEN I guess it's that I introduced and came out with a slightly different style, and that a lot of people have picked up on it.

GW The song "Eruption" changed everything practically overnight.

VAN HALEN Well, that's kind of what I'm saying, that I changed the way people played the guitar, you know? I mean, you see everybody doing it, and they weren't until I did it. So it's kind of obvious. It's not like I'm on an ego trip or anything.

GW What's your take on the L.A. band scene nowadays? How has it changed since you played the clubs?

VAN HALEN I think, in a funny way, that Van Halen kind of paved the way for that, too. When we were playing the clubs, there was no room for a bunch of long-haired, platformed, goofy-lookin' fools! [*laughs*] It was real hard for us to get into the clubs. It was always [*in gruff voice*], "You're too loud, your guitar's too psychedelic, etc." We used to get fired because you'd have to play five sets of Top 40 stuff, and we'd only have one set—which we'd play for the audition. We'd get the gig, play our one set of Top 40 songs, and then start playing our own stuff. Halfway through the second set the club owner would be screaming, "Hey! Get the hell outta here!" So we'd have to start playing our own gigs.

GW A lot of bands do that nowadays—the self-promotion thing.

VAN HALEN I'm not really too familiar with the club scene today. I don't even know where to go if I want to go to a club. I don't get out much.

GW There's the pay-for-play thing happening.

VAN HALEN Like at [*Los Angeles club*] Gazzarri's? I heard about that. You have to pay to play?

GW Bands have to pay something like $1500 to play.

VAN HALEN I'll tell you, making 75 bucks a night isn't much better! [*laughs*] It sure isn't enough to buy equipment. I mean, Alex and I used to go around and paint house numbers on curbs to make extra money.

GW Who are some of the players that have impressed you during the past decade?

VAN HALEN Well, there's Satriani and Vai. They're excellent players. [*pauses*] I don't really listen to anything! I'm always wrapped up doing my own stuff, always writing.

GW Any lesser-known players?

VAN HALEN Well, there's this band I'm producing called Private Life. And Danny Johnson, I love the way he plays. He's got that Louisiana blues sound, but he can also have the fire of Allan Holdsworth. He's got the vibe I really like.

GW One of the things you pioneered was two-handed tapping.

VAN HALEN I don't know if I was the first one to do it. I mean, I'm sure that somebody else thought of it, too! [*laughs*]

GW Nevertheless, people equate Van Halen with pyrotechnics. You brought it to the masses.

VAN HALEN Right. Funny thing is, I think I've mellowed out in my old age. I see a lot of people using it as a trick, but to me, it's just the way I play. It's not like, "Oh, oh, I'm gonna do a trick now!" I mean,

"Whether I tap or not, I'm still a good player."

you see these other guys playing and it's, "Watch this!" A trick. Like a vibrato bar—I don't use it as a trick, but as a way to play. I think I've gotten a little tastier through the years. I don't play as recklessly; I'm a little more melodic. I guess I'm much more into songs and songwriting.

GW Does it bother you that people have focused so much on the two-handed tapping technique? That maybe some other aspects of your playing have been overlooked?

VAN HALEN Yeah. I mean, whether I tap or not, I'm still a good player. If that's all I'm known for, then goddamn...

GW There are so many technicians around now, people who can really wail. But there are very few sonic innovators—people whose sound is instantly recognizable.

VAN HALEN I think that comes with time. When I first started playing, I was like—"brrrrrrrrr!"—as fast as I could go, too. It was fun. But as you mature a little bit, you see there's no point to it, and you start using your technique to bring out your style.

GW When did you notice that you were progressing on the guitar a little faster than your peers? When did the term "guitar hero" begin to be tossed in your direction?

VAN HALEN Probably when our first album came out.

GW But before then, there must have been people who said you were a pretty hot player.

VAN HALEN Well, yeah, when other people tell you, sure. Okay!

GW You've always acknowledged the mistakes on Van Halen albums. What are some of the most amusing examples?

VAN HALEN All kinds of stuff! I don't think there's any one song of ours that's done right all the way through. [*laughs*] Sometimes I'm out of tune a little bit. I heard "Where Have All the Good Times Gone?"

on the radio the other day, and I'm doing these harmonics...missed 'em. I kinda chuckled.

GW But most people would've removed their mistakes.

VAN HALEN Especially nowadays. Everything's so technically advanced. I'm not really a perfectionist, in that sense. I'm more for a vibe.

GW There was a pretty good goof in your cover of "Oh, Pretty Woman." You forgot part of the bridge.

VAN HALEN Yeah. I screwed up! [*laughs*] I never bought the record, I didn't know how the song went, so it was, "I think this is how it goes," you know? And so we did it, and realized later that it was wrong. I met Roy Orbison at Farm Aid. I don't even know if he knew we did it. You know, everybody was pushing for cover tunes on *Diver Down*, so I said, "Well, let's at least do 'Pretty Woman'—it's got a riff, unlike some of the other stuff we were doing.

GW Did you intend to go right from "Intruder" into "Oh, Pretty Woman"?

VAN HALEN Oh, that was an afterthought. We'd done the video for "Pretty Woman" and needed something else for it, so we went in the studio and just tagged that on. I was drinking a beer—that's me sliding the can on the strings—"A-rooo! A-rooo!"

GW Van Halen's sound on your first couple of records was very much that of a raw, live band. But this has changed somewhat. Now it's a fuller, more produced sound.

VAN HALEN Yeah, well, the main thing in the beginning was that I had never been in the studio before. I remember asking Ted Templeman and Don Landee, "Hey, do you mind if I just play like I do live?" Because I didn't have any rhythm parts underneath the solos. I didn't know how to overdub. That's why it sounds live—it is!

GW What noticeable changes have you made in the way you now lay down basic tracks?

VAN HALEN See, a lot of times I'll still do a live solo, but I'll just over-dub the rhythm part underneath. I guess we're just getting better at recording. The technology has advanced so much since '77!

GW Do you think your guitar sound has changed any?

VAN HALEN Believe it or not, I'm using the exact same stuff I always have. I have an old baby Marshall. And Kramers, which I started playing around five or six years ago. I don't know, I just turn everything all the way up! I used to use those old MXR Phase 90s on all the solos—it's kind of a cool sound. I don't use that much now, though. I have a rack that looks like computer shit, but I don't even know what's on it. [*pauses*] The only thing I use is a little bit of delay and a couple of Harmonizers. It's not a real tight echo.

GW You've been successful for some years now. How do you fend off complacency, the whole "rock star" trip?

VAN HALEN See, all I do is make music. I don't go out. I just sit up here on the hill, in my studio. I've always been that way, so nothing's different. A lot of people want to be successful so they can go out and party and have fun. But to me, making music is the fun part. I'm a weirdo! [*laughs*] I mean, that's what you saw out there [*points in the direction of the studio*].

GW "Beat It" created such a buzz. How did your involvement with that song come about?

VAN HALEN Quincy Jones called me up to ask if I wanted to play on Michael Jackson's record.

GW Of course, at the time, Michael Jackson wasn't the pop icon that he is today.

VAN HALEN I didn't think he was. But when that record came out, it sure was a big one! It was really funny. I was out back, and something was wrong with the phone. And you know, there's always people calling me. So I said, "Hello?" And there was this guy answering, "Hello?" We couldn't hear each other, so I hung up. And then the call came again: "Is this Eddie? It's Quincy, man!" And I'm like, "Who the hell? What do you want, you asshole?" [*laughs*] So finally he says, "It's Quincy Jones, man!" And I'm thinking, Oh shit—I'm sorry, man. It was really funny. After the record, he wrote me a letter thanking me, signed, "The Asshole." [*laughs*]

GW Did you work the solo out before you cut it?

VAN HALEN No, I just noodled along. I actually changed part of the song, though, because they wanted me to solo over the break. So I said, "Can we edit it to a verse, so there's some chord changes?" Then I just soloed over what I thought should be the solo section. I did two solos, and they picked the one they liked. That was it. It took about 20 minutes to do. And there was Michael, standing in the back saying [*mimics Michael Jackson*] "I really like that high fast stuff you do!" [*laughs*]

GW It seemed logical to assume that as of result of "Beat It" you'd receive a lot of offers to play on other people's records. Yet we haven't seen you do much of that.

VAN HALEN Yeah, well, just recently Stevie Nicks...Steve Perg... everybody's calling. Thank God I have an answering machine! [*laughs*] Believe it or not, I did the Michael Jackson thing because I figured nobody'd know. I swear to God. The band—Roth, my brother and Mike—always hated me doing things outside of Van Halen. They'd say, "Keep it in the band." And it just so happened that Roth was on one of his Amazon jungle trips or whatever he does, and Al was out of town, and Mike was out at Disneyland or something, so I couldn't consult them. So I just said, "Damn it, I'll do it and no one will ever know." So then it comes out and becomes song of the year and everything. My brother still won't let me live it down. And I did it for free, too! [*laughs*]

GW What about Tone Loc sampling "Jamie's Cryin' "?

VAN HALEN [*Excitedly*] Oh, right! I'm sitting around watching MTV one day and I think, That sure sounds like my guitar and Al's drums...

GW Wait a second. The story I had from the label is that you were consulted.

VAN HALEN Hell, no! I was just sitting there, and I hear my brother's drums. And then there's my guitar! So I called up our manager and said, "What is this shit?" So I guess he called them up and said that they should at least thank us. [*laughs*] And I guess we're thanked on the record.

GW This is done all the time these days. A lot of rap uses hard rock and heavy metal guitar samples.

VAN HALEN I think it's a bullshit thing. I mean, why don't they just have someone else play it? It's kinda thin, you know?

GW Let me ask you about your hearing. Does Pete Townshend's problem cause you any concern?

VAN HALEN Well, I'll tell you one thing I don't do, and that's stack my cabinets. Even in the old days, when I used to have the mountainous shit, I only used the bottom cabinets. Just don't stand in front of the stuff. I like to stand in front of them so I can feel my arm hairs move—but not the hair on my head.

GW You mentioned Satriani and Vai earlier, but did anybody else who came up during the Eighties make you sweat—maybe just a little?

VAN HALEN No. See, nobody makes me sweat. If anything, when I hear somebody good, it inspires me, you know? Like when I first heard Holdsworth, that made me want to play! To me, music isn't a competitive thing. There are so many good players around—I'm not in competition with them. I'm not out to be better than anybody. Music is such a personal thing. How can you say someone's better than someone else?

GW Well, there is some lame stuff out there.

VAN HALEN [*laughs*] That's true!

GW You were pretty involved with Holdsworth's career for a while there.

VAN HALEN Yeah, I got him signed to Warner Bros. because I just hated to see this guy who's so amazing selling guitars to stay alive. So I got him signed. I was supposed to co-produce the record with Ted Templeman and Donn Landee. Then—I hate to say this—while we were on tour in South America he just didn't wanna wait like two weeks, you know? So he did it himself...and it ended up being just another Allan Holdsworth record. The guy needs direction, you know what I mean? We did a couple of demos before I went to South America, and one of the songs was great. So he blew it, I think. I really think I could have, well, not necessarily pulled him back, but steered him in a different direction, you know? I was just over my friend Steve Lukather's house, and he played me Allan's new record, and I tell you, I couldn't tell the difference between that and his other records. I don't wanna rag on the guy, because he's an incredible player and he's a good friend. I love him. He just needs direction, that's all.

GW Have you worked with him since that episode?

VAN HALEN Yeah, I talked to him on the phone about a month ago. He called and asked if I'd want to do something with him. And I'd love to, except I don't really have the time right now. When the time is right, sure. It'll be fun. I don't give a damn if it's good or not. Like that thing I did with Brian May; that wasn't good, but it was fun.

I'd sure like to see how Holdsworth does some of his stuff, but I never had the nerve to ask him. It takes me two hands to do what he does with one. I don't know how he pulls it off! I mean, I have a hell of a reach, too, you know? I'd also love to pick Jimmy Page's brain about how he got some of those sounds. It'd be more in terms of sounds than, "How'd you play this?"

GW How do you feel about Page these days? He's been getting a bad rap.

VAN HALEN And that's bullshit. He's a genius. He's a great player, a songwriter and producer, so there you go. Put it this way: he might not be the greatest executor or whatever, but when you hear a Page solo, he speaks. I've always said that Clapton was my main influence, but Page was actually more the way I am, in a reckless abandon kind of way.

GW Do you still tinker around, building guitars, as you used to?

VAN HALEN Not as much as I used to. The only reason I did that was because I was trying to find—well, not necessarily the perfect guitar, but the guitar that served my means. I'll show you... [*Eddie exits, returning momentarily with his famous striped Strat with the Kramer neck.*] It does exactly what I want it to do. I used to build guitars because I wanted one that had a Gibson sound, but with a vibrato bar. I wanted a Strat with a Gibson sound, and that's what this is.

GW A lot of guitar manufacturers have taken cues from you over the years.

VAN HALEN Oh, God, tell me about it.

GW The non-pickguard. You were about the first to...

VAN HALEN The whole vibrato bar, one-pickup thing was my idea. It was actually a mistake, the way I came up with it. I bought a Strat, and took a chisel to it to carve out the rear pickup cavity, the one by the bridge, so I could drop a humbucker into it . But as I removed the pick-guard and put the new pickup in, I didn't know how to rewire it—you know, I couldn't get the wires back in. So I thought, Wow, I wonder how it'll work just straight to the volume knob. So I left it like that. Then I made myself a plastic pickguard to cover up the holes, and that's how this concept was born. You know, when I used to play Les Pauls I could never get a good sound out of the front and rear pickups at the same time. If you get a nice fat sound out of the back one and then you put it on the front, it's real muddy. Either that or you have to set it so bright to get a good sound out of the front one that the back pickup sounds like shit. So I just said, "Damn, what do I need two pickups for?"

GW You don't strike me as a real EQ freak or anything.

VAN HALEN Oh, no. I just turn everything up! [*laughs*]

GW If you turn everything up with some Marshalls, there's either too much treble or too much bass.

VAN HALEN Yeah, that's why I use the old ones. Any time I see an old one, I buy it. Even if it sounds like shit, because they can be made to sound good.

GW Is the Variac still a part of your sound?

VAN HALEN Yep.

GW Does that actually change the voltage?

VAN HALEN Yeah, that's all it does.

GW And you plug the output of the amplifier into the Variac?

VAN HALEN Yeah. That's all. It's a light dimmer! I use a studio light dimmer. See, it enables you to play at a lower volume, but you can still get the balls of the amp. I blew out the house once, when we used to live in this little shack in Pasadena. We had this little light dimmer in the wall, and I thought, Wow, I wonder what'll happen if I hook my amp up to that?

GW Once the Variac is installed, you just lower the dimmer and run the amp up full—it acts like a master volume control, and does so without your having to lower the master volume control on the amp.

VAN HALEN And you get the whole output of the amp. Know what I mean? It sounds sweet.

GW What do you think of the guitar sounds we're hearing today? What do you think when you turn on the radio?

"If I had to learn to read music, **it would take forever.**"

VAN HALEN I think everybody sounds the same. Playing-wise, too. Everybody has a Marshall stack now, and a guitar like this [*holds up his guitar*] or a Les Paul. Nobody's doing anything different. It all sounds like razor blades coming at your ears after a while. Just fuzzed-out noise.

GW What if you were a kid today, and there's already an Edward Van Halen out there. What would you do to avoid sounding like a carbon copy?

VAN HALEN I don't know...maybe pull out some old Cream records. Listen to old blues stuff and get your feel happening, instead of just jumpin' in and playing as fast as you can, copying the latest hit on the radio. I mean, I don't know what scales are—I just play what sounds right to me. I never had a lesson in my life. So, this scale or that scale, I don't know. To me, you have 12 notes to work with, and whatever configuration you use is up to you.

GW But didn't you study music theory as a kid?

VAN HALEN I was supposed to. It takes too long to learn. I don't even like to read books! If I had to learn to read music, it would take forever.

GW So a certain amount of ignorance is bliss?

VAN HALEN I think the grass is green on both sides—as long as you don't get too caught up in that reading-the-chart syndrome.

GW What about someone like U2's the Edge, who doesn't have a whole lot of chops but still created an identifiable sound.

VAN HALEN He sure likes his echo, doesn't he? But see, there again, he's more of a songwriter, and that's where it's at. Expressing yourself in a song is a lot more wide open then. All these kids who are just gunslingers, they'll come around. You can't be doing that all your life—it's impossible.

GW Do you ever feel, in a very small way, responsible for the emphasis on speed-playing today?

VAN HALEN For kids playing like typewriters? Hey, that's not my fault! Maybe they cop the speed because they can't cop my feel. Maybe they shouldn't think so much. I don't think when I play. I get the basic parts of the song and then, when I start soloing, I don't think.

GW While we're on the subject of sound, "Finish What Ya Started" is kind of a departure for you.

VAN HALEN It's a direct Strat. It was just for fun. We actually set out and tried to do something different, something goofy, and it worked.

GW Is it too early to talk about what you might do on the next Van Halen record?

VAN HALEN Oooh. [*pauses*] Anything and everything. Sammy and I are already writing, and we're comin' up with some really neat shit.

GW Is there any format you follow when you write together?

VAN HALEN Uh, I come up with music, he calls me and comes up with a concept, an idea—God, I don't wanna give anything away here—and he'll inspire me to write something. And then when I do, I'll inspire him, in turn, to write the lyrics to it. And then we sit down together and work it out. Then Al and Mike jump in and say, "We don't like that!" [*laughs*] No, I'm kidding. We never really write in the studio. The studio's just where we go to record. I just sit around with my guitar and a little cassette machine.

We've never had the luxury to do what we're doing right now, and that is stockpiling a bunch of tunes and then when we're ready to put it out, putting it out. Because with *5150*, you know, everybody was wondering what was going on with Van Halen, so we released it. And with *OU812*, we were already committed to do the Monsters of Rock tour [*with Scorpions, Metallica, Dokken and Kingdom Come*] before the record was even done. We would have preferred to finish the record, put it out, waited a bit, made sure we liked the record, and then booked a tour. That's what we're going to do this time.

GW How do you feel today about the Monsters of Rock tour?

VAN HALEN A lot of people slammed us for it, but we sold a lot of tickets. Not all of them were sold out, but hey, they were stadiums. That same year, Aerosmith and Guns N' Roses did the same thing, and they only sold like 30,000 seats outdoors. I didn't hear anybody raggin' about that.

GW You received so much flack about playing keyboards. Do you think people still don't see you as a keyboard player?

VAN HALEN I love playing keyboards, man. I write a lot of stuff on keys. It's like they don't want to realize that I play keyboards. See, here's the thing: when Dave was in the band, he would say, "Hey, man, nobody wants to see you play keyboards!" And I felt like, "If I wanna play keyboards or if I wanna play tuba, I'll play it."

GW Are you as much a tinkerer with keyboards as you are with the guitar?

VAN HALEN Nah. I just like fooling around with sounds. I love the old OB-8s because they're hands-on, you know? You can just turn a knob and change the sound. You don't have to be a computer whiz. Nice, thick sound too; I think they sound better than the digital stuff.

GW People associate you so much with note-heavy solos, but your solo in "Dreams" is surprising: for roughly half the solo you play only two notes.

VAN HALEN Yeah. It just felt right. When I'm behind the console, overdubbing, I just say, "Hmmm, let's try this." If that doesn't work, I'll try something else. Sometimes I get a solo right off, and other times I'll be doing it all afternoon and...nothing.

GW Do you have much of a problem with writer's block?

VAN HALEN Sure, don't you? Sometimes things just don't come. So I just walk away from it. Actually, sometimes, I'll try and work through it. I'll get pissed off and think, I gotta beat this thing! But other times it doesn't work. There are no rules. Sometimes it can happen for you, sometimes not. Put it this way—if you're up for 24 hours and getting nowhere, it's time to call it quits.

GW Van Halen has, of late, enjoyed a good relationship with the rock press. But up until *1984*, it seemed like you guys couldn't do anything to get a good review.

VAN HALEN I think they just realized that we're here to stay, you know? It's like a roach that won't go away. Finally it's, "Okay, stay!" It used to bother me, because some of these guys didn't know what they were talking about. If you don't like what someone does, then say you don't like it—but don't say it stinks. I mean, who are they to say something isn't good? At least say that you just don't like it as a personal preference, an opinion.

GW One thing rarely pointed out is the band's ability to sing some wonderful background vocals. Does that bug you?

VAN HALEN That's a unique part of the Van Halen sound. That's Michael and me. I don't really care if people comment or not. That's just the way we are, that's part of the sound.

GW A lot of bands just can't sing.

VAN HALEN It's true! The thing is, I'm not a singer, but I can hit a note. I have good pitch. Endurance is tough. Two beers, three songs, and I'm out.

GW Do you think Michael Anthony has gotten a short-shrift from the press?

VAN HALEN Sure. Because he's not a showboat kind of guy. Part of the reason I stick out so much is that Mike doesn't steal the show. I mean, if he wanted to hog the show, so to speak, we'd be butting heads. And if we tried to do unison things, what would be the point? I like the guys on the three instruments to be playing their own thing; I don't want everybody doing things together. The counterpoint thing, that's what I like. Just like the old Cream jams: they were all in their own worlds, but it worked.

GW Let's look ahead 10 years. Do you see yourself doing the same thing, with the same band?

VAN HALEN Oh, yeah. Definitely. I'm totally into family, so to speak. There's no reason why I can't be doing the same thing. I just want to make music and have fun. As long as you have the fire and you still want to do it, fine. When it starts getting old to me, then I'll start doing something else. I don't know what—maybe a race car driver!

[11]

"Whenever I try to plan something,
it never seems to work out."
—*EDDIE VAN HALEN*

LORD OF THE STRINGS

With his spanking Ernie Ball guitar and Peavey
amp in hand, Edward Van Halen struck a blow
For Unlawful Carnal Knowledge.

BY BRAD TOLINSKI

"**TURN LEFT! WATCH** that curve!" Associate Publisher Greg Di Benedetto can't contain his annoyance at my feeble attempts to navigate the treacherous mountain road that leads to 5150, Edward Van Halen's legendary home studio in Los Angeles. "You idiot," hisses Di Benedetto. "Pay attention to the damn signs! You fool, don't you know what happens to New Yorkers who lose their way in the vicious outback of the Hollywood Hills? Buzzard bait!"

My first instinct is to reprimand the man for his sharp-tongued babble. But his frenzied expression makes me think twice. It's not good policy to mess with a serious Van Halen zealot—particularly when barreling down the Baja at 87 M.P.H. in a unstable Galaxy 500.

The rabid bastard will probably rip my lungs out.

"Errruption! ICE CREAM MAN!" roars my twisted compatriot. I seize the exclusive map of "L.A.'s 10 Holiest Sites," presented to me by the people at Tanquery Liquor, and search for Van Halen's 5150 studio. To my consternation, I discover that this greatest of shrines has somehow been excluded. I conclude that the directory is probably the work of silly misfits and drunkards, and toss the offensive booklet out the window in disgust.

Suddenly, my companion points and bellows like a walrus hit by a stun gun. I jam the brakes and receive a mouthful of gritty road dust for my pains. By Divine Providence, we have miraculously stumbled upon the entrance to Eddie's rambling estate. Di Benedetto gasps, awe-struck: "Eldorado!"

We chug up a small hill, past Ed and wife Valerie Bertinelli's palatial Tudor-style house, and pull into a deserted driveway situated in front of a small, hut-like building: 5150. Di Benedetto and I leap from the car and gaze reverently upon the birthplace of "Hot for Teacher."

5150 is hardly the last word in opulence; the newly expanded studio looks rather bland—something like a large tool shed. But no one feels let down. We are, after all, standing in the presence of the temple of distortion, the grand mosque of two-handed tapping and devastatingly heavy squealing. Maureen O'Connor, Van Halen's super-efficient publicist, appears and leads us inside. You can tell Maureen's a pro—she politely pretends not to notice my partner's imbecile grin, and responds with stoical forbearance when he stubbornly insists on singing a brief hymn as we enter the studio.

As we explore 5150's dim interior, Di Benedetto roughly squeezes my shoulder when he spies the king's ancient Marshall. Flanking the legendary 100-watt head are two of Edward's recent acquisitions:

a purple Soldano and a new, prototype 5150 Peavey head. We are dismayed that he would use anything other than his Super Lead, but who are we to question the ways of Ed? Van Halen, we whisper in agreement, works in mysterious ways.

Unfortunately, there is little time to gawk, and we are quickly hustled to a privileged spot behind the band's new API recording console. Maureen places a tape of *For Unlawful Carnal Knowledge* into a DAT machine and pumps the volume up to vicious, cornea-popping levels.

Producer/engineer Andy Johns (Led Zeppelin, Rolling Stones) and producer Ted Templeman (David Lee Roth–era Van Halen, Doobie Brothers) have done a hell of a job in capturing the band's explosive rhythm section. Alex Van Halen gives the performance of his life, tossing off a bizarre array of tom fills with deadly precision. And the grievously underrated bassist, Michael Anthony, is finally riding high in the mix. But the biggest surprise is Edward's brutish, guitar-army approach on tracks like "Pleasure Dome," "Spanked" and the single, "Poundcake."

At the tape's conclusion we are escorted to the studio's lounge.

"Hey, man!" says an energetic figure sporting red Converse sneakers and a huge grin. Edward Van Halen hops over and enthusiastically shakes our hands, oblivious to our disheveled condition—and gaping mouths. "Howzit goin'?"

Van Halen unpretentiously settles into a battered antique barber's chair, takes a drag on his cigarette, and quietly asks what it is that *Guitar World* wants to know.

GUITAR WORLD This is the dawn of a new era for you. You've just released a new album, co-created a new guitar and worked with a new producer in a revamped studio. Was this part of some grand design?

EDWARD VAN HALEN Believe it or not, no. We started our last tour in 1988 and ended it in Japan in February of 1989. We consciously took a whole year off, during which I barely touched the guitar. We saw each other socially, but we didn't do any work. Then in the early part of last year, we sat together and discussed what we wanted to accomplish and everything just started falling into place. I don't want to spoil anybody's fantasies, but we rarely calculate anything. In general, we don't think that much.

GW What was the first order of business?

VAN HALEN Finding a producer. The name of Andy Johns, who produced most of Led Zeppelin's records, came up. Coincidentally, I had just met him in a recording studio while I was finishing production on the latest Private Life album. So we auditioned him.

GW You auditioned Andy? He's worked on some of rock's greatest albums.

VAN HALEN We needed to know whether we would get along with him on a personal level. Also, we wanted to see how he worked in the studio. All we knew was that he's made some great records. So we called him exactly one year ago today. He answered his phone and said [*assumes a growling, pub-drenched English accent*], "Hey mate, what do you want me to do? Come in and mess around a bit? No problem, but it's my birthday and I'm kind of hammered. Call me back tomorrow." He sounded like Dudley Moore in *Arthur*. And as it turned out, Andy is so rock and roll it's ridiculous. He really fit in.

GW What did Andy's audition consist of?

VAN HALEN We asked him to come around. At first he insisted on a second engineer, but we had to nix that idea because the studio is so small. So he came by himself. We started miking up the drums, and by the end of the day we were convinced that he was our man. He took control without being obnoxious.

GW Did you have any music prepared at that point?

VAN HALEN Absolutely nothing. That was the next big problem. [*laughs*] I wasn't really prepared, because I thought it would take a while to find someone we wanted to work with. The guys were asking me, "Hey Ed, you got any licks?" A little panicky, I said, "Hell no! Give me...uh...give me until tomorrow."

"Playing together without having to compromise our sound was **a dream come true.**"

The first thing I came up with was a real headbanger called "Judgment Day." It's a pretty simple tune. I figured, Gee, I haven't played guitar in a year, I can make it through this! [*laughs*] After that song was finished we continued to jam in the studio, and slowly the tracks started to materialize.

The whole record was done one song at a time. We'd completely finish one track before moving on to the next one. That's why there are so many different textures on this record. It wasn't done like our first album, where we banged all the rhythm tracks out in a couple of days. Interestingly, I think this is a much more powerful rock and roll record than our last two, despite the fact that it was conceived over a long period of time.

GW What did Andy bring to the record?

VAN HALEN He brought rock and roll inspiration. More importantly, he is the first engineer to capture the sound of Van Halen's rhythm section. The bottom line is: if Al is happy, then I'm happy. It isn't hard to get a great guitar sound. It's much harder to get a fantastic acoustic drum sound—which I think Andy did.

GW What modifications did you make in the studio?

VAN HALEN We installed a new, warm-sounding API console, which was custom-fitted for our relatively small room. It's got 36 inputs and features GML automation, which made it much easier to mix. We also added a drum room that practically doubled the size of the studio. The additional room really helped Alex capture the sound he always wanted. In the past we had to resort to Simmons drums because there was no way to isolate an acoustic kit when we wanted to play together—there just wasn't enough room. Playing together without having to compromise our sound was a dream come true.

We really took our time on the actual recording process, and made sure each one of us was happy with the sound of our instruments. In a way, it's the ideal Van Halen record.

GW Did Andy make suggestions regarding the arrangements?

VAN HALEN Not really. Wait, let me rephrase that. What I really appreciated about Andy is that he gave me space when I needed to develop an idea.

GW Why didn't you use engineer Donn Landee this time?

VAN HALEN We weren't unhappy with Donn, but we've done eight records with him and felt it would be nice to get a different spin on things. It wasn't any big deal.

GW What was Ted Templeman's role on this record?

VAN HALEN Ted came in to save the day last January. We thought we should try to finish the record. Since none of us are very good at finishing things, we thought of Ted. He is—and if you read this, Ted, please don't take it the wrong way—a very organized cat. I mean, you put Andy Johns, Sammy Hagar, Alex Van Halen and Mike Anthony and me in a room together, and we'll piss up a rope for years, just having fun and experimenting. Ted finally said, "Enough is enough. What do you want, a double record? You'll be here for another year. Let's finish what we've got." He cracked the whip and pulled everything together. He also worked on a lot of the vocals with Sammy, while Andy and I worked on guitars and guitar overdubs.

GW There are a lot of overdubs on this record, which is somewhat unusual for you. "Poundcake," for example, features a complete wall of sound.

VAN HALEN It wasn't really planned, it's just the way everything evolved. I came up with a riff that didn't really excite anyone until Andy suggested I use some electric 12-strings to flesh out the rhythm tracks. It turned out to be just the thing the song needed. All of a sudden, the lyrics, the title, everything came into sharp focus. What you hear are two electric 12-strings doubled under my usual dirty guitar.

Earlier, you asked what Andy Johns brought to this record. That was it—the inspiration that comes from the sound element. He would make a small suggestion, or move a knob or two, and our sound would change, automatically goosing our creative juices.

GW What kind of 12-string did you use?

VAN HALEN It's a guitar developed by Roger Giffin, who works out of Gibson's custom shop. We worked together on my Steinberger guitars. His custom-12 has these small Smith pickups that look like something between a single-coil and a humbucker.

GW On the solo in "Poundcake" it sounds like you were using your new neck pickup.

VAN HALEN You're right. It was like, "All right! I've got a new toy!" The neck pickup is all over this record.

GW It also sounds like you dug your old wah-wah out of the closet. You use it quite a bit.

VAN HALEN People always ask me what I was thinking. I wasn't thinking! It was pretty spontaneous. A wah-wah happened to be floating around the studio, I plugged it in, and that was that. And I think that because it was handy, I used it on several tracks.

GW You function on a very intuitive level, just by letting things flow.

VAN HALEN Whenever I try to plan something, it never seems to work out. So why plan? It only seems to lead to disappointment.

GW You've owned 5150 for quite a while now, and it's just a stone's throw from your house. I imagine that you tinker around. Have you grown more studio-sophisticated?

VAN HALEN I know how to run the shit, believe it or not. Actually, this is kind of a touchy subject. In the old days Donn Landee kind of monopolized 5150. He was the only one who really knew how to run anything. It was his gig, so he was very protective and didn't want anyone else touching the knobs. Andy is just the opposite. He showed me how to run the console and seemed more than happy to receive my input. It was a real relief to finally know my way around, because I could go in and record ideas at any given time. I actually got to the point where I could punch myself in with my toes! I think my wife also punched me in on a couple of things. It was like, "Honey, when I count to four, push record!" My recording setup is so simple—you know, two Shure SM-57s on a Marshall cabinet—that it really wasn't any big deal.

GW How do you mic your cabinet?

VAN HALEN Two mics on the same speaker—one directly in the middle and one angled from the side.

GW Why the angled microphone?

VAN HALEN At one point Andy complained that he wasn't hearing enough bottom. So I said, "Okay, okay, then put another mic on the speaker." That's the way we solve problems in the studio. A lot of it is just common sense.

GW This record is probably the most sonically varied and adventurous of your career. "Spanked" epitomizes this new experimental approach.

VAN HALEN Again, it's totally unconscious. I didn't set out to make this an experimental record. For example, the guitar-like bass line on "Spanked" is a total fluke. One day Andy walked in with a Danelectro six-string bass, and I thought, Oooh, that's neat. I plugged it into my Marshall and it sounded wild. It just seemed appropriate for the main lick in "Spanked."

GW But it seems to me that if you're using a new guitar and are in the process of developing a new amp, at some point you must have consciously wanted to experiment with new sounds.

VAN HALEN I'm not after a different sound; I'm just trying to find the epitome of what I've always heard in my head. Initially, the only reason I co-designed the new guitar was that Sterling Ball had been hounding me to do it for over a year. He was after my ass! Fender wanted me, too. At one point, all these guitar companies came out of the woodwork because I wasn't working with Kramer anymore. I went with Sterling because his company did a fine job with my 5150 strings, and I was confident that he would do good work.

At first, I really wasn't sure if I wanted to put my name on another guitar. The initial step was to see if I could come up with a body shape that I liked; once I got over that hump, it just snowballed. But to get back to your point: I wasn't searching for something different. I just have a natural curiosity that varies from day to day. If I started the album today, I'd probably approach it in a completely different manner.

GW When you played with Steve Morse and Albert Lee in Anaheim, California, at the beginning of the year, you used a Soldano head onstage. Now you're developing a new amplifier with Peavey. Why?

VAN HALEN Again, it's just fine tuning. Look, the Ernie Ball/Music Man guitar isn't very different from my original guitar, except that it has a front pickup designed to complement my back pickup. One of my major frustrations is that I've never been able to find a front and back pickup combination that sounded good together. I've never used a front pickup because they've never sounded good with my setup. And if I got the front pickup to sound good, then the back pickup would sound like shit. DiMarzio's Steve Blucher and I worked hard to remedy that situation, and I couldn't be happier with the results. The key is that both pickups are completely different, and if you swapped them it would sound really wicked—simply awful.

GW But back to the amp.

VAN HALEN It starts with the guitar, goes through the cord and then into the amp. Hopefully, the amp will reproduce what the guitar is designed to do. That's what I'm interested in. I made some previous attempts to have an amp designed for me, but they fell through. One day Hartley Peavey flew me down to his factory in Meridian, Mississippi, with the intention of getting me to use one of his guitars. I told him I didn't need a guitar, but it would be cool if they could design an amp for me. They agreed.

Next, Peavey flew a real nice, down-home Southern guy named James Brown out to California to work with me for a couple of weeks at a time. He'd tinker away, then ask me what I thought. I'd say, "That's not quite it, how about adding another tube." And so on.

It's a pretty serious research and development trip for me, and the amp is starting to sound pretty damn good.

To tell you the truth, I don't care how many amps they make or sell. I just want a line of dependable, great sounding amps for myself. I don't give a damn about the rest.

GW So what's so special about the Peavey amp?

VAN HALEN It's very straight-ahead—it doesn't feature chorusing or anything like that. It's just balls-to-the-wall. It's got five different preamp tubes, and each gain stage is set up so you get the ultimate amount of sustain without too much fuzz. For once in my life I don't have to rely on a Variac. It's really a hot amp. It hasn't blown up on me yet, so I'm really jazzed. We're working on a cabinet, but I'm still waiting on it. For now, I'm running it through my standard Marshall cabinets.

" **Something always goes wrong** during the course of a show. "

GW Why change amps? Your legendary Marshall, which you've used since *Van Halen*, sounds incredible.

VAN HALEN I'm not sure whether it's that my tastes have changed or if the amp has changed, but I think that my Marshall is starting to fade—it just doesn't sound like it used to. Even Donn Landee started noticing it. So I guess it was time to start looking elsewhere.

GW It must have been frightening to rely on that old Marshall, knowing that it could blow at any minute.

VAN HALEN And believe me, it has!

GW It's always been rumored that that amp was heavily modified.

VAN HALEN That's bullshit, man! The guys in the band used to say, "Don't tell anybody what you use." I took their advice, but I never really lied that blatantly. [*chuckles slyly*] Basically, I just let people believe what they wanted to believe. The only thing I've ever done is use a Variac to lower the voltage to about 89 volts, so I could turn the amp up without blowing it up. It's been re-tubed, but basically it's just a stock amp.

The bottom line is I really think that every guitar sound comes from the player's fingers. I must've told this story on countless occasions: one time Ted Nugent wanted to play through my magic black box—until he found I didn't have one. When he played through my rig, it still sounded like Ted.

GW Did you use your Marshall for a reference tone when developing the Peavey?

VAN HALEN No, my reference was my ear. It depends on what side of the bed you wake up. I mean, I just played through the Peavey earlier today and thought, Hmmm, this sounded better yesterday.

Occasionally, when I'm recording and can't get the sound I want out of it, I'll just turn the studio monitor down so that all I hear is the unamplified guitar. And I'll lay the parts down that way.

GW Why isn't there a Van Halen live album?

VAN HALEN What's the point?

GW Yours is one of the few groups that could make a legitimately great live record, because the band is so spontaneous.

VAN HALEN I've never heard a tape that I've been completely satisfied with; something always goes wrong during the course of a show. It usually isn't until the last show of any given tour that we finally elimi-nate all the bugs. I'm always yelling at the road crew for something. It's always, "Sorry, we'll nail it next gig." And we never do until the last couple of shows, which are usually perfect. Then the comment is something like, "Don't worry, we'll nail it next tour."

Anyway, there's really no such thing as a truly live album. I don't know of any live record that hasn't been doctored in some way, unless you buy a bootleg. Even Cream doctored their stuff. Andy Johns told me that "Crossroads" was not one take. He swears that it was put together. I wasn't there so I can't say for sure, but I've heard the same thing from several reliable sources. On the other hand, who cares? It's still great. Let's put it this way—Clapton played it.

GW Do you ever put solos together via punch-ins in the studio?

VAN HALEN Hell, yes! I admit it, I'm not proud. "Jump," for example, was punched in. You can hear that there are two distinct parts to that solo. I can't even remember what I played originally. All I remember is the recorded, pieced-together version that everybody knows.

GW Let's talk about some of the tunes on the new album. The solo on "Judgment Day" sounds premeditated.

VAN HALEN Yeah, it wasn't a wing-it thing; it was definitely something I set out to do. It's a double-handed thing that I used to do in my live guitar solo. I just took part of it and inserted it. The actual body of the solo is a kind of surf thing that I came up with.

GW How many takes do you usually do?

VAN HALEN No more than three.

GW Do you keep them all?

VAN HALEN No, and that scared the hell out of Andy. I'd say, "Man, I can beat that take. Just record over it." Andy would always look at me very suspiciously and say, "Ohhh, Eddie, I don't know..." [*laughs*] But really, I never worry about it, because a solo ain't gonna make or break a tune. A solo should just highlight a song.

GW "Spanked" is frightening. It really stomps.

VAN HALEN It's actually kind of a joke tune. I mean, c'mon, it's about getting spanked! Let me tell you where the title of that song comes from: Anyone who has ever spent any time in 5150 complains about the placement of our monitor speakers. They're strange because the room used to be a racquetball court—it wasn't designed to be a recording studio. So Andy Johns walked in for the first time and said, "Hey, mate, your speakers sound kind of spanked." "Spanked!" That killed me. When something is beat to shit, it's "spanked." We quickly adopted it into our vocabulary, and Sammy wrote a song about it. I think that's the funniest song on the album, but nobody seems to get it. It's such an odd combination of heavy music and goofball lyrics. A week ago Mo Ostin, the big cheese from Warner Bros., came up here. He listened to that track with a puzzled look on his face, stroking his chin and saying things like, "Gee guys, that's er...nice."

GW Both "Spanked" and "Pleasure Dome" sound as though they're influenced by Led Zeppelin.

VAN HALEN It's funny you should mention those songs together, because Al really helped to shape both tunes. He's a total Zeppelin freak, so it's not surprising. I don't mean to downplay Andy's influence, but I think Alex had more to do with the Zeppelin-esque touches. He's a very musical guy —he's not just a drummer. In my book he's the baddest. He was the one that suggested using the E-Bow at the beginning of "Spanked." And "Pleasure Dome" would not be on the album if not for Al. At one point it was just three disjointed riffs. He helped me bridge them together.

GW You and Alex have always had a tremendous musical affinity. Are there any areas where the two of you don't mesh?

VAN HALEN I'm always screwing around with time, because I never count. The solo in "Poundcake," for example, goes: four bars, another four bars, then two bars. Al kept insisting that it wasn't finished. He likes to count, and I never do. I'm strictly feel.

GW "Right Now" has an almost gospel feel to it.

VAN HALEN I can hear Joe Cocker singing that one. I wrote that music quite a while ago, before Sammy joined the band. If there was any other vocalist I'd like to make a record with, it would be Joe. That song has that classic "Feelin' All Right" groove.

GW What about "316"?

VAN HALEN That's something I've had for quite a while as well. I played that to introduce my solo segment on the last tour. I also play it a lot to put my son, Wolfy, to sleep at night. The guys dug it and wanted to put it on the record. I decided to call it "316," because that's Wolf's birthday. I used a Gibson Chet Atkins acoustic solidbody steel string on it. I ran it directly into the board and effected it with an Eventide Harmonizer.

GW "On Top of the World" features the riff you used in the fade-out to "Jump."

VAN HALEN Wow, you noticed that! I almost didn't put that on the record, because everything else seemed so new and fresh. Andy forced me to put it in. He kept saying, "I love that song. You have to put it on the record." I used my "Hot for Teacher" Gibson Flying V and my Marshall on that tune, which was cool. But, to be honest, we had five other tunes that I would've preferred to use that didn't make it to the album.

GW "Pleasure Dome" features that clean-but-dirty sound.

VAN HALEN That was the Steinberger. But there's the difference between what you call "clean" and what I call "clean." That's almost too clean for me. I consciously went for a different sound on that one, because I was using the Steinberger Trans-Trem and it would have sounded too muddy if I used my usual amount of distortion.

GW But when you analyze it, your sound is not really that distorted.

VAN HALEN That's true. In fact, a lot of times I'll have friends around and they'll ask me to dirty up my sound. I prefer a cleaner, more open sound with sustain to a dirty sound that just sounds scratchy and buzzy.

GW "Pleasure Dome" also features one of your very best solos ever. Was that spontaneous?

VAN HALEN It's an overdub, but I just winged it.

GW "In and Out" is very bluesy.

VAN HALEN I think that my overall approach on this album was much more bluesy and traditional. There's not as much of the wacky tapping stuff. Sometimes I almost feel embarrassed for coming up with that shit!

"God gave me one big bottle
of alcohol and I drank it real fast."
—*EDDIE VAN HALEN*

CUT AND DRY

Edward Van Halen trims his hair, quits drinking
and regains his *Balance.*

BY TOM BEAUJOUR WITH GREG DI BENEDETTO

EDWARD VAN HALEN welcomes me to 5150, his legendary 24-track home studio, with a handshake and a slap on the back. But for a split second I am unable to return the warm greeting, as I am dumbstruck: standing in front of me, it seems, is not Edward, but his evil twin.

The guitarists moppish hair has been lopped off, leaving in its place an expertly styled flattop. Van Halen's soft-featured face, once frozen into a perpetually boyish grin, has been hardened by a newly sprouted goatee. When I gather the courage to ask what prompted this drastic makeover, Edward's response is amiable.

"I lost a golf bet with [*Buffalo Bills quarterback*] Jim Kelly, and ended up having to shave my head with a fucking Norelco razor," he explains. "I just decided to leave it short, because I was sick of having long hair."

The fact is, Edward is a changed man in far more significant ways than his choice of 'do. For the most part, the guitarist has abandoned the pyrotechnic guitar antics that rocketed him to prominence 17 years ago, opting instead for a more lyrical, restrained approach to his instrument. More significantly, Edward, who will turn 40 in January, is the father of a three-and-a-half-year-old son, Wolfgang, and he takes his role as a parent extremely seriously. Unlike many celebrities whose involvement with their children extends only to child-support payments, Edward lovingly subjects himself to the unglamorous but rewarding rigors of everyday parenting. "Wolfie wakes us up at six in the morning, saying, 'Come on, you're mine, Daddy. I want to do this. I want to do that,'" he says with a doting smile. "I take him to school every morning."

No sooner have I dispensed with the pre-interview pleasantries when Edward whisks me into the studio's control room. As he prepares to crank up the band's soon-to-be-released album, *Balance*, on the studio's ear-annihilating monitors, Van Halen pauses, his finger poised on the CD player's "play" button.

"You know," he says with a concerned look, "you should probably listen to this in the car because it sounds much better in there. We mastered this record differently than the last one, and it sounds more ballsy—except in here."

Tempted as I am by the offer to hang out in one of Edward's many fine automobiles, I politely decline, opting to remain in the more spacious and well-lit environment of the control room. "Well, okay," says Eddie. "Here we go!"

The album opens with an ominous Tibetan monk chant sample which gives way to the lush, heavy layers of "Seventh Seal." Suddenly the music stops. "You have to listen to this in the car," says Edward. "It really sounds better."

Moments later, the two of us are seated in what must be the Van Halens' new family car, a charcoal-gray Mercedes sedan. In spite of the vehicle's austere looks, the stereo system is brutally loud, and *Balance*'s wave of guitar goodness swallows us alive. Edward sits quietly, his eyes closed as he basks in the glory of his own creation. Periodically, he wakes from his deep-listening trance to point out a particularly noteworthy lick or explain the origin of a song. Apparently, Van Halen's success has not lessened the mixture of excitement and apprehension that he, like most musicians, feels when unveiling a just-completed piece of work.

Consistent with Edward's new-found maturity are his most recent efforts to put an end to his well-documented drinking habit. "I think that God gave me one big bottle of alcohol and I drank it real fast," he says. "God gives everyone a bottle when they're born, and they have to make it last a lifetime. Well, I drank mine too quickly, so I just can't drink anymore."

Surprisingly, Edward, who will consume several non-alcoholic beers during the course of the interview, is more than willing to discuss the topic of his drinking at great length.

Although it may come as a shock to some, hard rock's perennial whiz kid has become a man.

GUITAR WORLD Was all of the new album recorded here at 5150?
EDWARD VAN HALEN Almost everything was done here, except for five lead vocal tracks, which were recorded in Vancouver.
GW Why did you go there?
VAN HALEN Because Bruce Fairbairn, our producer, lives up there. He would fly down every Monday morning and we'd work during

the week. On the weekends, he'd go home. We had promised him before we began recording that we'd do some vocals up there so that he could be with his family a little more.

GW It seems awfully adult for Van Halen to be sticking to the kind of rigid recording schedule you're describing.

VAN HALEN Bruce is very structured. He wouldn't let us loaf for a minute, so we completed *Balance* more quickly than any other album we've done in years. We wrote, recorded and mastered the whole fucking thing in five months. We started in June, and by the end of October it was mastered.

GW What kind of pre-production work did you do to prepare for the recording of *Balance*?

VAN HALEN We demoed about 20 songs for Bruce. Actually, we over-cut! There are like four songs that aren't even on the record. It just got too long. We had an hour's worth of music in the can, and Bruce said, "Do you want to do a double CD or what?"

GW How did you decide which songs should go on the record?

VAN HALEN Well, out of, say, 20 songs, the ones that got finished first ended up on the record.

Sometimes, when I focus on writing, I start blazing: I'll come up with all kinds of shit and it overwhelms Sammy for a bit. The way he works best is when he focuses on one thing and writes lyrics for it. So, since I was writing so much, a lot of lyrics weren't done. For example, for the instrumental track, "Baluchitherium," we were actually working on lyrics and we ended up going, "Fuck it, it sounds pretty good without vocals," so we left it. And Sammy was relieved— "Okay, I got one less to work on." So, yeah, there are actually four more tunes that the music is finished for. We'll finish those for the next record, or whenever.

GW Even though you made the album so quickly, the song arrangements seem more thoughtfully developed than anything you've done in the past.

VAN HALEN Yeah, they are. Bruce just said, "Work, motherfuckers." He's a serious guy. He walks in with his briefcase and says, "This is what we're doing today." We would be like, "Oh fuck, I don't want to do it. Let's do that tomorrow." He always answered, "No, you're doing it now." [*laughs*] It was great working with him. We're doing the next record with him, too.

He's a very musical guy. He dabbles in a little bit of everything, plays a little guitar and a little piano, but his main instrument is trumpet. He's producing Chicago right now—a big band horn thing. Bruce isn't like certain producers who spend all their time on the phone and every once in a while ask, "Got it yet?" He's a hands-on guy.

GW Were you at all worried that Bruce, who produced Aerosmith's last couple of albums, might make the band sound too slick?

VAN HALEN No. A good producer brings out the best in the artist he's working with. You shouldn't be able to listen to something and say, "So-and-so produced this album." Bruce's stamp is not on our record because a good producer should not have a stamp. People who are only capable of molding a band to fit their "trademark" sound are bullshit producers. Bruce, on the other hand, just enhanced the best parts of what the band already had to offer.

GW Van Halen recording sessions have in the past been fueled by large quantities of alcohol, but drunkenness and dissipation don't seem to be compatible with Bruce's disciplinarian production style. I notice that right now, at least, you're drinking a non-alcoholic beer. Are you not drinking at all anymore?

VAN HALEN No, I'm not.

GW How long has it been since you stopped?

VAN HALEN It's been off and on. This time about a month. Actually, I did really well while we made the record. I played a lot of stuff sober, which really weirded me out. It took me a while to get into it without the help of the alcohol.

GW What is it about drinking that facilitates your playing?

VAN HALEN There's like this wall, and when I drink, my inhibitions are lower so I just wing stuff without getting embarrassed or nervous. But I have to get past that because drinking's no good. I've been doing it too long.

GW Do you have any insight into why you've had so much trouble stopping?

VAN HALEN Because I can't stop! I'm an alcoholic. It's like, "Just a couple? Fuck you! I'll drink until I go to sleep."

GW Your father had a drinking problem as well, didn't he?

VAN HALEN Yes, but I think my problem is more a product of my environment than any genetic factor. I remember my dad got me drinking and smoking when I was 12. I was nervous, so he said to me, "Here. Have a shot of vodka." Boom—I wasn't nervous anymore. My mom used to buy me cigarettes and it just stuck, it was habit. I don't drink for the taste of it, I drink to get a fucking buzz. I like to get drunk. I really do.

GW Do you think that the fact that your work schedule is less rigid than most people's has resulted in your drinking more?

VAN HALEN You know, believe it or not, I drink more when I'm playing and writing and working than when I'm not. I come up to the studio and drink and work. When I go into the house, I don't drink. If I spend a weekend at the beach, I don't drink. So it's really funny.

GW It's definitely uncommon.

VAN HALEN For me, leisure time is not the problem area. My problem is that I go to the office to drink. It's completely ass-backward. And the only reason I keep doing it is because it still works, believe it or not. It just breaks down the inhibitions. And I'm too inhibited, ordinarily—I get real nervous.

GW You said you recorded most of *Balance* sober.

VAN HALEN Yeah, but sometimes, I would listen back to something and go, "Ooh, that's stiff. Let me redo that."

GW Uh-oh.

VAN HALEN But I didn't drink too much. When we made the last record, I had at least 12 to 15 beers in me each day. This time, nobody but me drank while we were working. And if I got a little bit overboard, I'd say "I'm out of here, I'm too far gone," and call it a day.

Do you know what I've noticed that's funny? When I'm really tired, I feel the same as when I'm drunk, because it's easier for me to get through to the other side, or whatever you want to call it. It's easier for me to just let go and not judge what I'm doing. It's all about just opening up and being free. But if I'm drinking I don't even think about it. It's like, "Oh, I made a mistake, big fucking deal."

GW Overall, *Balance* seems to be a darker record than *For Unlawful Carnal Knowledge* and its immediate predecessors. What inspired you to write the music?

VAN HALEN I don't really know what inspires me to write the music I do, but usually, the music will set the tone for the lyrics. I don't think it's really that dark. The first tune, "Seventh Seal," is kind of that way, but "Can't Stop Loving You" is an awesome rock groove.

GW There are more songs written in minor keys than on the last record.

VAN HALEN D minor. Everything's in D minor, the saddest of all keys.

GW While we were listening to the record a little while ago, you indicated that you recorded the strange piano piece, "Strung Out," back in the early Eighties.

VAN HALEN Yeah, I forget exactly what year that was, but it was before '84. Valerie [*Bertinelli, Edward's wife*] and I had rented [*popular composer, pianist and arranger*] Marvin Hamlisch's beach house for the summer. I just used to waste this beautiful piano. It was like a Baldwin or a Yamaha. It had cigarette burns all over it and I was sticking everything but the kitchen sink in it: ping-pong balls, D batteries, knives, forks—I even broke a few strings.

I don't know what prompted me to do it. I was just fucking around. Actually, it started off with me playing the strings with my fingers. I would create harmonics by hitting the key and muffling the string up and down to bring harmonics out like on a guitar. I have like 10 tapes of this stuff, and Bruce picked out this little part. He loved it.

GW Was Hamlisch furious when he returned to his house?

VAN HALEN Yeah, he was. I tried to get the piano fixed before he came back, but he found out somehow. I guess they didn't repaint it as well as they could have.

GW You feature an acoustic guitar very prominently on "Take Me Back," one of the tracks off the new album. What finally prompted you to go "unplugged," if only for a moment?

VAN HALEN I actually wrote that ditty a while ago. I wanted to put it on the last record, but we never really completed it. This time around I really wanted to finish the song, because I still really liked it. So we worked it up.

GW What kind of acoustic did you use?

VAN HALEN It's a South American guitar called a Musser. I bought it at [*L.A. vintage shop*] Norm's Rare Guitars.

GW Other than using an acoustic, did you do anything else out of the ordinary for the album?

VAN HALEN Nope. As usual, I have two Shure SM-57s miking one cabinet. Pretty much everything was recorded with the 5150 amp, but I did use the old Marshall Super Lead head on about three tunes. The stuff that's real clean-sounding, like "Aftershock," was done with the Marshall.

GW Why did you decide to use the Marshall again?

VAN HALEN Just to get a different sound.

GW A few years ago, you were convinced that the amp had faded beyond the point of usefulness.

VAN HALEN I think I just got tired of it. Just recently, this Dutch guy named Peter cleaned the amp for me and restored it to its totally original state. Even though I never had the amp modified, a bunch of parts had been replaced over the years.

I've also got a Peavey 5150 combo unit coming out in January. It's 60 watts and has two 12-inch speakers and a sealed back. It's a bad-ass little amp. It just shits all over every other combo on the market—at least in my opinion. I've been working on the amp for the last year because I wanted it to have a really good clean channel, because most people who want a combo amp need it to be versatile.

Of course, I wanted the main sound to be happening, as well. That also took a lot of work, because the amp's electronics had to be packed into a smaller box, with the controls on top. When you start changing wire lengths around like we had to, it usually affects the sound, so it took Peavey's tech, James Brown, a while to perfect it.

GW Even though this record has a drier sound than *For Unlawful Carnal Knowledge*, the guitars still have that chorus-y shimmer that's become a staple of your sound lately. Do you double most of your rhythm tracks?

VAN HALEN No, not at all. But everything has the Eventide harmonizer on it. The dry guitar signal is on the left, and the duplicate sound that the Eventide generates is on the right. I barely use the harmonizer as an effect; it's just to split my guitar to both sides of the stereo spectrum. I have it set to detune to 98, so it harmonizes just a little.

GW When did you start splitting your signal like this?

VAN HALEN I think *Fair Warning*, or the album after. Maybe *5150*. I forget. But that's been my thing ever since.

In the old days, Donn Landee [*engineer on every Van Halen album from 1978's* Van Halen *through 1988's* OU812] would have my dry signal on the left and a little echo or reverb on the right. And I'm going, "Well, why don't we use the harmonizer and get the whole fucking guitar over there instead of just [*makes breathy noise to imitate the decay of a reverb or Echoplex unit*] the tail-end of everything I play. I hated that sound.

GW Really? I always thought of it as a really cool trademark of your sound.

VAN HALEN I can't stand it. I guess it worked for the first record. But after that it got old really fast. If you have a car and the left speaker's blown, the guitar is gone. If you're sitting on the right in the back seat, you don't hear the guitar even if both front speakers work. What kind of shit is that?

GW It sounds like you have your guitar plugged into a Leslie on "Not Enough."

VAN HALEN We plugged the Marshall into the Leslie via this preamp box that my tech, Matt Bruck, brought over. He had used it on the demo tape for his band, Zen Boy. He hooked me up and I just played it.

GW What inspired the solo on that song?

VAN HALEN I was hearing a Beatles-ish feel, so I went for a "While My Guitar Gently Weeps" kind of thing.

GW The songs on *Balance* seem to have more key changes than your previous work.

VAN HALEN It's called "better songwriting." [*laughs*]

GW Has your piano training given you an increased understanding of harmony, which in turn helps your songwriting?

VAN HALEN Yeah, totally.

GW You play some barrelhouse piano on "Big Fat Money," but besides that, there aren't very many keyboards on *Balance*. Is there a reason for that?

VAN HALEN Yeah, I haven't really spent that much time playing piano lately. I think that old synth sound didn't feel right for this record. I might use it in the future, though. Who knows.

GW "Big Fat Money" has an unusual solo that's almost humorous. What prompted that radical departure from your usual style?

VAN HALEN That was Bruce's idea. He's going, "Hey, let's go for a jazz sound." And I'm going, "Okay." So I pulled out an old 335, ran it through my Marshall set really low and just did it. It's funny.

GW At the end of the instrumental track "Baluchitherium," there's an entire menagerie of guitar sounds.

VAN HALEN That's exactly what it is. It sounds like a bunch of animals—like a zoo. There's a bunch of birds and chirps and dinosaur calls and the elephant sounds I've always made. It just felt like a fun thing to do. You can even hear my dog Sherman howling on there.

GW What mic did you use on the dog?

VAN HALEN Uhhh, a Sennheiser. [*laughs*] We have pictures of it too; it's so funny. We had to tape a hot dog to the microphone. Swear to God. The dog was afraid of the mic. We kept pushing him up there and he'd back off. So we taped the hot dog to it, and then started making a bunch of noise. We actually bought a tape of a fire engine. We'd play the tape, and Sherman would get up to the mic, sniff the hot dog, and bark.

GW In addition to the dog and the other animals, it also sounded like there was some six-string bass on that song.

VAN HALEN Actually, no. You know what I used? It was a Music Man Albert Lee model guitar that I strung with heavier strings and tuned down to low A.

GW What does "Baluchitherium" mean?

VAN HALEN Actually, Valerie tipped me to it. When she heard the song for the first time, she said, "That sounds like a dinosaur song," because it sounds so big. She started looking through a book and said, "How about 'baluchitherium?' " And I'm going, "What the fuck is that?" I started reading, and it turns out that the baluchitherium was the biggest mammal that lived in the prehistoric age. Valerie always titles songs. She titled "1984."

GW It's surprising you don't really solo over the track, since there are no vocals in the way.

VAN HALEN I just wanted a simple melodic feel. Even if there were to be a solo, it would only diverge from the melody a little bit. A lot of times, if there's a melody there, I prefer to stick to it, or maybe play with it a little, as opposed to indulging in gymnastics.

It comes back to the same old question people are always asking me: "When are you going to do a solo record?" Well, if I did, it would probably be similar to "Baluchitherium," meaning it would be Van Halen music—which I write anyway—but without singing. I wouldn't do all the loony gymnastic shit. What's the point? That stuff goes in one ear and out the other.

GW It appeals to a select group of people.

VAN HALEN Yeah, I mean, who can play the fastest, who can do this, who can do that. Fuck, who cares? I stopped doing that years ago. On this album, I focused on fitting the song. For example, on "Take Me Back" I did a little slide ditty that just fit the song, instead of playing an actual solo. "Seventh Seal" has no solo at all. Instead, I added a musical interlude that worked for the song.

On *Van Halen,* I was a young punk, and everything revolved around the fastest kid in town—the gunslinger attitude. But I'd say that at the time of *Fair Warning,* I started concentrating more on songwriting. But I guess in most people's minds I'm just a gunslinger. The thing is, I do so much more than just blow fucking solos. Actually, that's the least of what I do.

GW To what extent do you think the success of Van Halen still rests upon your skills as a guitar player?

VAN HALEN I have no idea. I don't analyze it. I try to concentrate on writing good songs and, hopefully, people will like them.

GW Have you ever considered leaving your unaccompanied solo out of your live shows?

VAN HALEN I've thought about it many times. Actually, back when Sammy joined the band, I said, "I'm tired of doing fucking guitar solos," but everyone insisted that I had to keep doing them.

GW Isn't it still a thrill for you to have people focusing on you alone and to hear them scream your name?

VAN HALEN Yeah, but it's such masturbation. A lot of it is just screaming, "Look at me!" Some parts of the solo, like "Cathedral" or "Eruption," are little compositions, and I don't mind doing those. But, still, what's the point? I get bored doing it.

GW In one of your previous *Guitar World* interviews, you said that sometimes you're a little embarrassed that you popularized the two-handed tapping technique, because it became such an over-used gimmick.

VAN HALEN I did feel that way, but I don't anymore, because nobody's tapping these days.

GW Even you don't tap as much as you once did.

VAN HALEN I do it as much as I always have. It's part of my playing. I used it all over the record; you just can't tell. I probably tap a little bit in every song. To me it's a part of my playing, it's not, "Oh, I'm going to do my trick now."

GW You recently lost your manager and dear friend, Ed Leffler, to cancer. How has his passing affected the band?

VAN HALEN I hadn't really thought about it. We've got a new manager, Ray Daniels, who also manages Rush, King's X and Extreme. We all miss Ed, but life goes on. I guess it brought us closer. Ed was never involved with any of the music, so when we're in the studio, actually making music, we don't think about him that much. It's just, you know, around his birthday and holidays and everything—that's when you think about him.

GW Did you take more control of your business affairs in the period of transition between managers?

VAN HALEN We had to—and, boy, it's a ridiculous job. I would never want to be a manager. You get at least 50 phone calls a day about totally stupid, ridiculous shit.

GW Were you criticized for "selling out" when you let Pepsi use "Right Now" for their ill-fated Crystal Pepsi advertising campaign?

VAN HALEN Probably, but the only reason we gave them the music was because they were going to use the song anyway. They would just have recut the song with studio musicians, like they do for some TV movies when they redo an old hit because they can't use the original. If they use the original, they've got to pay, but if they don't, all they do is give credit to the artist and then pay the studio cats. Pepsi told us that they were going to do that, so we said, "Hey wait a minute, we might as well get the money." I ain't that proud, you know. I'm not going to say—"No, go ahead, rip us off. And keep the money too!"

GW What's a day in the life of Edward Van Halen like?

VAN HALEN I spend time with my son, Wolfie, and play a bit of golf.

Actually, I started to take some lessons last week, because I'm still a hack at it. I don't get out there enough. It's a cool game for life, because when I'm fucking 90, I could still be doing it, so I might as well learn how to play now.

Our whole road crew plays, so on the road, you get to hang with the guys—which is an awful lot of fun. Golf isn't really about hitting the ball, it's more about male bonding. Letting it hang.

GW Does your son, who you seem to spend much of your time with, play an instrument yet?

VAN HALEN He likes to beat on Al's drums and he loves piano. The other day, actually, Valerie and I were up above the garage where I keep all of my guitars, looking for something, and Wolfie saw all the guitars and said—he was so decisive—"You know, when I get bigger, I'm going to play the guitar." [*laughs*] It's like, "Okay, take your pick." He said it with such conviction!

Actually, he isn't exposed to that much music because I really don't play in the house. You figure that he'd be doused with music from the minute he wakes up until he goes to bed at night, but no. He has a normal kid life: he watches Barney and Mickey Mouse and all that shit.

GW So you try and make sure that Wolfie leads a normal life?

VAN HALEN No, it's just that I'm normal. I don't do anything that out of the ordinary. He hates loud noise so he'll come in here and go, "Daddy, too loud. Too loud!" Yeah, he makes me turn the shit way down. It's really funny.

GW He knows that you play music, but do you think he understands your "unique" situation?

VAN HALEN I don't think so. I don't think he's got that yet. Sometimes, I'll say, "I'm going to work now, Wolfie," and he answers, "You mean you go to the studio?" Then he comes here to visit me when I'm trying to write, and I'll be sitting here with my thumb up my ass, smoking cigarettes and plinking around on the guitar. To him, that's what Daddy does for work. He'll put it together later, I guess, but right now he probably sees other people going to work whereas I just take the golf cart up here.

GW He probably tells his friends at school, "My dad drives a golf cart." Has he ever seen you play live?

VAN HALEN Oh yeah! He loves it. He's walked out onstage before, not knowing that he really shouldn't. We'll be standing there jamming, and he just walks out. I was doing my guitar solo once, and I was playing "316," which I wrote for him. He came running out while I was playing, and the crowd just went nuts. I thought to myself, Whoa, fuck man, I must be really putting some muscle into this or something, because normally they don't cheer that loud for this section! It turned out they were cheering for him. He had the spotlight on him and he was grooving!

GW Are there aspects of your celebrity that you dislike?

VAN HALEN Everyone feels like they own a piece of you, and it's like, "Fuck you! You bought the record, right? That's what you own; you don't own a piece of me!"

GW Do you get recognized as soon as you leave the house?

VAN HALEN Well, not since I cut my hair. Nobody recognizes me. It's great. Unfortunately, as soon as the album comes out, everyone will know what I look like again.

It comes with the territory. I'm not pissing and moaning about it at all, it's just that you're asking me. It bothers me a little when I'm having dinner with my wife and someone comes over to our table and says, "I really don't mean to interrupt you or bother you..." Just give me the piece of paper so I can sign it, and get the fuck out of here!

One particular episode comes to mind. I was on a plane, headed to do Jim Kelly's "Kelly for Kids" benefit, and this lady asked me for my

autograph. I asked who it was for, and she answered, "Say 'To Cindy.'"
So I wrote "To Cindy" and my name. She looks at me and says, "Well,
I could have done that!" I go, "Well, what the fuck do you want?" Did
she want me to write her a book?

GW Some people seem to have more problems coping with fame than
others. Do you think that the constant public scrutiny was one of the
causes of Kurt Cobain's suicide?

VAN HALEN If it was, then why was he in this business? Why didn't
he just give all his money to charity and live normally? I think it's so
funny how bands say, "We don't want fame and fortune." Well, what
do they do this for then?

If you want to be a true artist, then make your music and don't
even release it. Put it this way: if fame had Cobain crazed to the point
where he offed himself, then he went too far. He should have stopped.

I think the guy was just on drugs, man. I think it was drugs. I don't
think he was thinking straight. He was fucked up. It was terrible, man.
That's the worst karma a person could have—to off himself. I mean, did
he want to come back as an ant, or a fucking turd or something? It actually
pissed me off when he did that. He wrote great tunes, and if nothing else,
he deprived a lot of people of what he could be doing in the future.

GW Since we're on the topic of drug use, you mentioned that you
weren't absolutely thrilled about Sammy's choice of topic for the
song "Amsterdam."

VAN HALEN Well, the song is about smoking dope, and I thought
the music might have warranted something more...metaphoric. I
envisioned something else, but since I don't write lyrics, I'm not one
to piss and moan about it.

GW Did you ask Sammy to try and come up with something different?

VAN HALEN Yeah, but he liked it, so that was that. You know, he doesn't like everything I do, either. We're not going to fight about it to the point where the song doesn't get put out. It's part of being in a band. You work together, and you can't please everybody all the time.

GW Now that you're a father and a role model for your son, does it bother you to have songs about drugs on your records?

VAN HALEN No, not at all. I don't support any kind of censorship. There's just a time and a place for everything.

GW Have you been approached to do *MTV Unplugged*?

VAN HALEN Yeah, but I'm not an unplugged kind of guy. I don't want to sit there and try to play our music on an acoustic guitar. What's the point? I didn't write it on acoustic—I wrote it on electric guitar, and that's the way it's meant to be delivered. If I wanted it to be acoustic, I would have done it that way originally. I'm not going to butcher my music just so I can be the flavor of the month.

GW What's the best thing about being Edward Van Halen?

VAN HALEN It's a great feeling for people to like what you do. I do what I like and other people like it. It's a great payoff. How many people get to experience that?

The other day, I was playing golf on a public course in Pasadena with these two old timers, and one guy says, "Shit, man, a bad day on the course is better than any good day at work." And I started thinking, Well, I guess for you, but I like my work. I'm really lucky, because I really enjoy making music. I don't consider it to be like clocking in and doing a job.

I'm not making light of making music either. It's hard work, but I enjoy what I do—creating something as opposed to making a part for a fucking Impala or something. I'm just lucky to have found that. And that's half of it: me enjoying what I do. The other half is when other people dig it. That's like, "Whoo! Home run!"

REPRINTED FROM *GUITAR WORLD*, DECEMBER 1996

[13]

"I don't think I've done anything. I feel like I'm just starting."
—*EDDIE VAN HALEN*

ERUPTIONS

Dave isn't the one, Sammy's cryin' and Eddie's
hot for Gary. Right now, life seems pretty
complicated for Van Halen.

BY STEVEN ROSEN

ONE OF THE FIRST things you notice upon entering the maintenance room of Edward Van Halen's 5150 complex is a series of five Polaroid snapshots, arranged vertically along the edge of a doorway. Four of these depict Edward sitting atop a 5150 combo amp, grinning aimlessly, as if the photographer was simply testing the settings on the camera. The fifth picture captures the band—Edward, brother Alex, Michael Anthony and Sammy Hagar—in cozy, smiling camaraderie, their arms draped around each other's shoulders. Most striking about this print, however, is the fact that someone has plunged a yellow push pin through Hagar's face. The perfect placement of the pin indicates that the deed was about as accidental as the assassination of Lincoln. No, this is nothing but bad Van

Halen voodoo, mean mojo stuff—an act of venom and doom.

By now, only the brain dead are unaware of the changes that have rocked the Van Halen camp. Singer Sammy Hagar is gone, his solid gold locks nothing but a memory. David Lee Roth, absent for over a decade, returned to appear on a pair of new tracks available on the band's *Best of Volume 1* greatest-hits package, the band's first such compilation ever. But despite feverish speculation that the flamboyant singer would rejoin Van Halen, fate and, in all likelihood, Eddie, deemed otherwise: Roth is out, history for the second time. Of course, Van Halen had a powerfully felt reason to reject a reunion that would, if nothing else, been a diamond-studded cash cow for the group.

"We're from different planets; we don't communicate," says Eddie of Roth. "We just don't see things the same way. I'm not saying that he's a bad person at all—I actually fuckin' love the guy. But I don't need that kind of negative energy around me. I don't know how to explain it, but Dave kinda sucks the life out of me." So instead of David Lee Roth making a dramatic re-entry into the Van Halen fray, a dark horse candidate emerged and was handed one of rock's plum jobs outright—none other than the former Extreme frontman, Gary Cherone. Cherone, known for his acrobatic stage antics and extraordinary vocal range, impressed Eddie with his quiet manner: "He's like a brother. He's shy, he's a quiet guy and has no fuckin' attitude. He's just a beautiful human being. Plus, the guy sings and sounds like an angel."

Van Halen, who despises the politics of the music business as much as Roth revels in it, has, these past few uncertain months, endured a romp through hell without sunscreen. In an intimate conversation which initially began at his Hollywood Hills hideaway and three days later ended with a frantic game of phone tag, he shared with *Guitar World* his view of Van Halen's massive implosion, the too public upheaval that led to the ousting of one lead singer and the temporary resurrection of another. He also talked about the band's recent greatest-hits album, a work which in its depth reveals just how much rock's premier guitarist matured as an artist and as a man in the course of 20 spectacular, if turbulent, years.

GUITAR WORLD The last few months have been difficult ones for the band.

EDWARD VAN HALEN Yeah, the last three months have been a full plate—and a few desserts I didn't plan on ordering. There had been a variety of conflicts brewing between Sammy and the band since I quit drinking on October 2, 1994. Then things really came to a head when we began work on the soundtrack to the movie *Twister*. It got so bad that I actually started drinking again.

GW What were some of the more nagging issues?

VAN HALEN Well, in the last couple of years, Sammy went through a lot of changes; he divorced his wife of 23 years and, possibly because of that, stopped being a team player. He was especially irritated by the fact that I began to get involved with the lyric writing. Sammy would say, "You never complained about the lyrics before!" Well, I wasn't sober before, and I wasn't even listening to the lyrics!

It's not like I suddenly wanted Sammy to be my puppet or anything, but once in a while, I would take issue with a specific lyric or line. For example, I always hated the words to "Wham, Bam Amsterdam," from *Balance*, because they were all about smoking pot—they were just stupid. Lyrics should plant some sort of seed for thought, or at least be a little more metaphorical.

GW So you really began to have problems with Sammy around the time of making *Balance*?

VAN HALEN I'd say that we actually had problems on every album except for *5150*. Sammy wouldn't even work with Andy Johns on *For Unlawful Carnal Knowledge*; he demanded to work with Ted Templeman, because Ted lets him get away with everything.

Then, like I said, things got really ridiculous when we started working on the music for *Twister*. Alex had called up the director, Jan de Bont, to ask him how closely he wanted the lyrics of the song that became "Humans Being" to be related to the content of the movie. De Bont said, "Oh, please don't write about tornadoes. I don't want this to be a narrative for the movie."

So we put him in contact with Sam, who called me and said, "I had a great conversation with de Bont and everything is cool." Then—maybe two seconds after I got off the phone with Sammy—de Bont rang me up and was like, "Uh, Sammy is a little strange. I kept telling him that he shouldn't write any lyrics about tornadoes, but he still kept insisting that I fax him tornado-related technical jargon. Does Sammy just want to learn about twisters for his own personal reasons?" I said, "Beats the hell out of me." And so what lyrics did Sammy come back with? "Sky is turning black, knuckles turning white, headed for the hot zone." It was total tornado stuff! Not only did Alex and I tell him not to do that, but the director of the fucking movie told him, "Do not write about tornadoes."

We had the music for the song completely done for six weeks, during which time Sammy had refused to fly to the studio from Hawaii, and suddenly the deadline was on us and we had no lyrics. So I was on the spot, and I came up with the title "Humans Being" and a melody. When Sammy finally decided to show, he, [*producer*] Bruce Fairbairn and I ended up writing the lyrics together at the last minute. Sammy sang the track in an hour, because he had an eight o'clock flight to catch. Sammy was long gone to wherever when I came up with the low, growling vocal part which I sang, "We're just humans/humans being," and he never heard any of that until the record came out. That's how into it he was.

The situation with Sammy was so bad that I had to warn Bruce not to let him know that I had come up with the title and the melody, because if he had found that out he would have completely turned off. Whenever I suggested something to Sammy, he would just stop listening to me.

GW There were a lot of rumors circulating that Sammy was unhappy with the band because he felt he was being forced into projects he didn't want any part of.

VAN HALEN Sammy was dead against the greatest-hits package, because he was afraid it would lead to comparisons between him and David Lee Roth. I said, "Wait a fuckin' minute, Sammy, this band has been putting out records for 20 years and never put out a greatest hits—but you already have two of them [Best of Sammy Hagar, *1992*; Unboxed, *1994*]!

It just goes to show you that in his mind, he was always a solo artist—once a solo artist always a solo artist. He was only into being in Van Halen for the prestige of it.

GW You've recently begun collaborating with super-producer Glen Ballard (Alanis Morissette, Aerosmith), who co-wrote the two new songs on *Best of Volume 1*.

VAN HALEN Glen is just the most beautiful guy you'll ever meet. I won't work with anybody else any more—there's no reason to. He and I connect, like musical soulmates. He wrote Alanis Morissette's album in one day, and he and I are that way, too. When we get together, we brainstorm and a song is done in two seconds.

GW What was Sammy's reaction when you started working with Glen?

VAN HALEN We had several band meetings with Sammy where we told him that if he wanted to continue with Van Halen, he had to stop running around doing all his solo shit and become more of a team player—which might involve collaborating on a lyrical level. He said, "No problem." We had another meeting to reiterate that after the premiere of *Twister*.

So right after that, we began working on this song "Between Us Two," because we thought it had amazing potential. Sammy Called Mike [*Anthony, bass*] one Sunday afternoon and said, "I heard that Glen has some great ideas for the song. I'm really excited." Then he called me Sunday evening to give me his fax number so I could fax over Glen's lyrics. And then, suddenly, in the middle of giving me the number, he just started yelling and screaming at me: "This is a fucking insult! I ain't gonna sing someone else's bullshit!" I was totally startled, like, "Wait a minute, we discussed this at length on two occasions. We didn't spring this on you, man." Finally I said, "Okay, forget the new lyrical treatment, but at least come down, take another pass at the performance and change a few lines." He just answered, "Yeah, well, whatever."

That's when I finally put my foot down. I said, "Sammy, if you're not here at the studio by six o'clock tomorrow, don't ever bother coming back." The next day, he showed up like nothing had ever happened—like he hadn't yelled and screamed at me. Did he think I was some idiot who didn't remember what had happened the night before? I'm sober now, dude.

Glen and I were sitting there working on the song, and the opening line was something like, "I want to see you/I want to know who you are"—kind of a *Dark Side of the Moon* vibe, the premise being, "I want to touch your soul, I want to get to know you." Then Sammy decided to change it to some shit like, "I can't see your diamond ring/through your shining star." I was like, "Sam, please, Glen's got some great lyrics here, just go with them." His only reply was, "If I thought those lyrics were better, I would sing them...besides, I have a plane to catch." And he just left. Glen and I were dumfounded. Then Glen asked me, "How long has this been going on?" I said, "Longer than I'd care to mention."

So anyway, that was the last straw. I called Sammy a bunch of times and, when he finally returned my call, I said, "Sam, if you want to make another record or do another tour, you've gotta be a team player. Van Halen is a band—not the Sammy Hagar show, or the Eddie Van Halen, Alex Van Halen or Michael Anthony show. We could be called Piss for all I care, but we are a band."

So I went over this shit like 11 times with him, and he finally said, "Yeah, goddamnit, I'm fuckin' frustrated. I want to go back to being a solo artist." And I said, "Thank you for being honest."

We ended up hanging up like everything was cool because it was all out in the open. He'd admitted that he wanted to do solo stuff. And I said, "Well, you can't be in a band and do that too, so see ya." I didn't fire him—he quit.

I'll put it very simply: Dave and Sam both suffer from L.S.D.: lead singer disease. Except Dave never lied.

GW Speaking of David Lee Roth, how did he come back into the picture?

VAN HALEN Dave happened to call me around the same time Sammy quit, because Warner Bros. had notified him that the greatest-hits package was going to come out, and he had a few questions about the packaging and other details like that. I told him, "Dave, I really don't know yet, I'll call you mid-week and let you know." We were on the phone for about 45 minutes and we apologized for things we had said back in high school—even junior high. It was probably one of the best conversations I've ever had with him. Especially since as long as I've known him, we were never really friends. We were just from different planets. But band-wise, it just seemed to work.

A few days later, instead of calling David with the information on the CD, I decided to drive over to his house. I told him that the basic idea was to do a single CD that would be half him and half Sammy. That was another big problem we had with Sammy, by the way; he wanted to have more of his songs on the greatest hits than Dave's.

GW What was it like going to Dave's house that first time?

VAN HALEN We just had a great time bullshitting as friends. We hung out for about three hours and smoked some cigars. It was only about two weeks later when I realized that the only new track we had for the greatest hits was "Humans Being," that I came up with the crazy idea of having Dave sing on a couple of new songs. We thought about it for a couple of days and said, "Yeah, why the fuck not?" So I called Dave and said, "Would you be interested?" and he said "Sure, I'm not doing anything." I was very clear that he was not in the band—that it was just a project. What I wanted to do was write five new songs and pick two out of those five.

We had a little bit of a difficult time because we wrote a song for him that he didn't particularly care for. It wasn't up his alley. So we got past that and Glen Ballard and I sat down with Dave, and I played him all this new material I had. Eventually we narrowed it down to this pop song, "Me Wise Magic," and a shuffle, "Can't Get This Stuff No More," with a "Panama" sort of groove. "Me Wise Magic" has a line in it, "I know what you're thinking," which Dave felt uncomfortable with. He said, "That bit sounds so angry; it's just not me. People want to hear Dave sing." But I thought it was majestic; it takes you on a roller coaster because there are so many changes. I nicknamed it "The Three Faces of Shamus" because there is that first low part, the high part, and then the chorus. All three have completely different vibes going on. At first he wasn't into that one at all. A week later I was still playing him songs and finally he said, "What about that first one?" So, finally, he came around and realized it wasn't as dark and angry as he originally thought.

During this process, Dave and I were really becoming good friends. In my heart I really wanted to believe that he had changed a bit. We worked and we worked and he actually thanked me for hanging in there with him. It was a struggle to find anything that would inspire him and that he could connect to. Finally we came up with the other song and Glen suggested the title and the premise of it. So Dave came up with the lyrics and it worked. But Dave said, "Thanks, because any-one else would have probably thrown their arms up and said fuck it." And I said, 'Well you're a trooper, however long it takes and whatever. It's about making it a good song. There's no time frame here, it doesn't have to be done tomorrow. I just wanted to find something you liked and I'm glad I found one."

GW So the two of you were able to put all of your past acrimony behind you?

VAN HALEN Oh, yeah, we were actually becoming friends. Before we went to the MTV Video Awards, we all sat down—[*Van Halen manager*] Ray Daniels, Dave, Al, Mike and I—because we knew we were going to get mobbed by the press. And it was actually Dave who said, "Let's tell the truth." Less to remember. And the truth is, we did two songs for the best-of, we did two videos, and that's it.

We could go out there and make a killing on tour with Roth, but we're not a nostalgia band. I would never just take somebody's money for playing old songs to bring back memories. Memories are memories to be left memories. If we ever did that with Roth, we'd have to write and record a new record and then play a few of the old ones. I'm sure a lot of fans would love to see it—but some things, like I said, are better left to memory.

GW So why aren't you making a new record with David? Was there some sort of fracture?

VAN HALEN Everything went to pieces at the MTV Video Awards. After we went out onstage to present the award to Beck, we started doing some interviews there, and I was just telling the truth—the way it is. I said, "If we do a tour we'll have to write and record—a new record. But before any of that can happen, I have hip replacement scheduled for December 16, and that's going to put me out of commission for at least four to six months.

After doing a couple of these interviews, Dave's attitude changed. I asked him what was wrong, and he said, "Well, what's with this hip thing? Would you stop mentioning the hip thing?" I said "Okay, no problem. In the next interview I won't say a word about my hip." He turned to me and said, "You fuckin' better not." And man, I lost it! I yelled, "You motherfucker, don't ever talk to me or anybody like that again. Don't bother calling me anymore."

I thought he had changed, but two minutes onstage and a half-assed standing ovation and he turned right back into the old Dave that I hated.

GW Who chose the tracks for *Best of Volume 1*?

VAN HALEN Ray and Al came up with a list and I just looked at them and said, "Yeah, fuck, I don't care." Because there's a second volume ready to go. There are a ton of other songs that people get pissed about when we don't play them live.

GW In previous interviews, you've said that you didn't want to do a greatest-hits album.

VAN HALEN I changed my mind. What's wrong with that? Valerie [*Bertinelli, Edward's wife*] is always on the internet, and for a lot of the people out there, their first exposure to the band was *Balance*. And when they find out we have 10 other albums, they're not gonna go out and buy 'em all. So why not put a package together so they can at least get a taste and a history of the band? Next year will be the 20th anniversary of the recording of our first record, so I don't see a problem with putting out a greatest-hits record—not as long as the next record we make is great.

GW What gear setup did you use on the most recent tracks?

VAN HALEN The meat and the beef of the sound is the 5150. And I did experiment with some new stuff—I used a talk box on "Can't Get This Stuff No More," but Matt [*Bruck, Van Halen's guitar tech*] actually ran it for me. My mouth wasn't big enough or something because when I tried it just sounded like a wah-wah. I played and then we added it later with Matt doing it through a re-amp or whatever you call it. On "Me Wise Magic" I'm using the prototype Peavey with the Steinberger tremolo.

GW During the period when you were in vocalist hell, did you think about maybe putting together a solo album of some sort?

VAN HALEN No, not at all. A long time ago, when Dave totally took us by surprise and just quit, we didn't audition anybody. It was Sammy and that was it. We were just excited to have somebody who was into singing. Actually, my plan at the time—and I wouldn't necessarily have called it a solo record because Mike and Al would have played on it—was to get Mike Rutherford [*Genesis*], Pete Townshend, Phil Collins and Joe Cocker, all of whom I had talked to. I had written "Right Now" back then and I wanted Joe Cocker to sing on it. It would have been fucking great. That's what I wanted to do, write a record where I did all the music and had a different singer on each song. Logistically, it would have been a nightmare—people on tour, contractual agreements, companies pissing and moaning—and we'd probably only be finishing it now. It would have been fun. Hopefully, in the future I'll still be able to do that.

GW Looking at *Best of Volume 1*, which provides sort of a capsule view of what Van Halen has done, makes me think: Did you have any sense 20 years ago of the volume of music you would create? Could you see down the road at all?

VAN HALEN Believe it or not, since I've gotten sober I don't think I've done shit. I don't think I've done anything. I feel like I'm just starting.

GW You say you feel like you've just begun, but the truth is, Van Halen is one of the few guitar-driven rock bands to still exist here in the Nineties. Most of the other bands who were around and thriving in the Eighties are gone.

VAN HALEN Let's just call us a rock and roll band. We just are what we are. I don't know how to explain it, we survived punk the first time around, we survived disco and grunge and rap and whatever. We're a rock and roll band and we just do what we do.

GW Do you worry at all about what your audience will think about the changes in the band, primarily the addition of Gary Cherone?

VAN HALEN No, because you cannot please everyone all the time. No matter who sings, someone is not gonna like it. I'm sick and tired of being controlled, and I don't want to control. I just have so much music and I want to put it out. Gary's very talented and we work very, very well together. We'll let *Best of Volume 1* run its course and then we'll put out the new shit. I don't care...if it touches one person, then it's great. I don't care if it sells millions, I don't care if it sells a tenth of the records that we've sold. It's not about that, it's for the love of music.

[14]

"I couldn't wait for the day
I'd be able to make music with my son."
—*EDDIE VAN HALEN*

LIKE FATHER, LIKE SON

Eddie Van Halen put the fire in the group that
bears his name. It took his son, Wolfgang, to
rekindle the passion and get the group on the
road for one of the most anticipated reunion
tours in rock history. In this world exclusive
interview, the father-and-son duo talk about
their relationship, working and performing
together, and the rebirth of Van Halen.

BY CHRIS GILL

IS MUSICAL TALENT genetically inherited? If your test sample is the Van Halen family, the answer undoubtedly would be yes and the proof would be the current Van Halen tour, which features the Van Halen brothers—Alex and Ed—on drums and guitar respectively, as well as Ed's 16-year-old son Wolfgang on bass. Although Wolfgang picked up the bass less than two years ago, his comfort on arena stages in front of crowds of 20,000 fans suggests that it was always in his DNA to be a performer.

Wolfgang's membership in the band may now seem like pre-determined fate, but Ed was careful from the beginning to let Wolfgang's musical interests and talents develop naturally, even though Ed often hinted that he hoped his kid would follow in his footsteps. "I'm going to let Wolfgang be whatever he wants to be," he stated in 1995 when Wolfgang was only four. "I don't see how he won't somehow be into music, being exposed to it all the time. But I'm not going to force him to play piano or take music lessons like my parents did to me."

Wolfgang's guest appearances on guitar during Van Halen's 2004 tour showed that Ed's kid had not only taken an interest in music but he had also quickly developed true talent as a musician. Even so, devoted fans were taken by complete surprise when Ed revealed in late 2006 that Wolfgang was Van Halen's new bass player. A few months later when news leaked that David Lee Roth was returning as the band's vocalist and a tour was in the works, critics wondered if Wolfgang was truly qualified. Playing one of the most anticipated tours of the past 20 years is a hell of a first job for anyone, let alone someone who was just 16 years old and never played in any other bands before.

What seemed like a risky move on paper proved instead to be an overwhelming success as Wolfgang breathed new life into the band with the right balance of youthful enthusiasm and devoted reverence to the band's classic songs, all of which were recorded several years before Wolfgang was even born. While the tour gives Van Halen fans an opportunity to see the band with David Lee Roth again, the presence of Wolfgang onstage opens the door to a new chapter in the band's history. What lies ahead in the future is anyone's guess, but with Wolfgang joining the band its foundation is now stronger than ever as is its potential to grow in new directions.

Talking with Ed and Wolfgang, several unusual qualities become evident. There's no generation gap between the two, but more im-

portantly they reveal an undeniable mutual respect and admiration
for each other that even Wolfgang's occasional rebelliousness and
Ed's playful displays of parental authority can't hide. The two are
truly in awe of each other's talents. One gets the feeling that Wolfgang would be a huge Van Halen fan even if his dad wasn't in the
band and that Ed would want to make music with Wolfgang even if
Wolfgang wasn't his son.

   With rave reviews coming in for the band's current tour and a lifetime of possibilities lying ahead to explore, the future for Van Halen
as a band looks very bright thanks to the addition of a new family
member. As the saying goes, the family that plays together stays together, and this family positively jams.

GUITAR WORLD How did Wolfgang join the band? Did you ask him
to join?

EDDIE VAN HALEN I asked him. We were in the studio one day, just
jamming on some stuff.

WOLFGANG VAN HALEN Actually there's a story behind that. It was
in the summer of '06. My dad said, "Hey, do you want to jam?" and I
said, "Sure."

ED I'll never forget it. [*to Wolfgang*] You played the blonde five-string
bass with four strings on it.

WOLFGANG Oh yeah!

ED It was the first time that he played bass.

   So, the drum room is in the back of the studio. Al was in there,
and he couldn't see us, and we couldn't see him. Wolfgang picked up
the bass and I put the bass in Al's headphones. It was the first time in
30 years that Al's had bass in his headphones. Al said, "Hey! How are
you playing bass and guitar at the same time?" I got on the talkback

and said, "Say hi, Wolfie!" and you went [*in high voice*], "Hi, Uncle Al!" Your voice was a lot higher then. Al went, "Who's playing bass?" I told him it was Wolfie, and it blew Al's mind.

WOLFGANG After that, Al asked if I wanted to jam again. I said, "Yeah!"

ED That's when I asked him if he'd like to be the bass player in Van Halen. He said, "Yeah, as long as I don't have to do a certain thing," which I won't mention. [*laughs deviously*]

WOLFGANG I can say that: I said, "Sure. I just don't want to do a bass solo."

ED Even though you do have a couple of solo spots that shows everyone that you are a world-class player.

WOLFGANG Yeah, whatever. Then we just made it a religious thing on every Wednesday and Saturday to play. We just kept playing relentlessly and eventually we thought, Hey, we're pretty damn good!

GW So in the beginning everything happened organically.

WOLFGANG We didn't lay out a plan or anything. It just fell together. We played together a good four months without any vocals, and we just looked at each other and knew it was awesome.

ED It's like Dave says, "Three parts original, one part inevitable." And it was inevitable.

GW Wolfgang, you play several instruments—guitar, drums, keyboards. What drove you toward the bass?

WOLFGANG Well, it was the only open spot. [*everyone laughs*] And the people filling the other spots—drums and guitar—are the two greatest players of those instruments in the frickin' world. I find the bass safe. You don't have to go out on the line.

ED I remember another thing you said at the very beginning: "Can I just groove?"

WOLFGANG I just like to be there to groove and keep the song going.

GW Your dad always says he wishes he was the bass player.

WOLFGANG I love being a bass player. It's just me and Al—a groove section. Just *boom, boom, boom,* and we're good.

ED He is so *on.* Hey Wolf, wanna switch gigs?

GW There *are* huge expectations on you, Ed.

WOLFGANG But you've got to admit that there were huge expectations on me before the first show.

ED Before we went on tour a lot of people were saying that Wolfgang got the gig just because he's my son. But after that first gig, forget it. It's just hands down, hands up, hands sideways: he's a musician and a Van Halen.

GW Was the time in between when the tour was announced and when you played the first show difficult?

WOLFGANG I just wanted to get it over with. I wanted to be where we are now. There was so much weight on my shoulders to fill the shoes and prove that I could do it. I *knew* I could do it, but I wanted to say, "Everybody, hey, I *can* do it!"

ED We rehearsed probably six months before Dave showed up. We were almost over-rehearsed. We got to the point where we were goofing around.

WOLFGANG That's when we started playing "Little Dreamer" in double time.

ED When Dave walked in it blew his freakin' mind.

WOLFGANG That night was magical. That was the first time I heard vocals with everything.

ED Dave couldn't believe how good you are.

GW Wolf you've gone directly from rehearsing with your dad and uncle to playing some of the biggest venues in the world. Was it difficult for you to make that transition?

WOLFGANG Because we rehearsed so frickin' much, from spending six months in 5150, then at Center Staging and then for a few weeks at the L.A. Forum, I felt that we had done enough preparation for me to feel safe. Plus when you're on the stage. you're far enough away from people that you feel comfortable. With the lights and everything sometimes I can just close my eyes and feel like we're in that room at 5150 again.

ED It's a lot different than rehearsing in the studio. It's probably more comfortable than being in the control room with a bunch of people staring at you.

WOLFGANG It's definitely a lot more open. That room is claustrophobic.

ED I've always said that the more people there are, the more chance there is that someone will like it.

WOLFGANG When there are only 10 people around, I get nervous. But when there are so many other people I feel more comfortable. Then it's just the four of us doing our thing.

ED If there's just one person and they don't like you, you're fucked. If you've got two people at least, there's a 50-50 chance that at least one of the two people will like you, hopefully.

GW How did your dad help you prepare for the tour?

ED The first thing I told him is look out for the bitches!

WOLFGANG He didn't really help me prepare. He just told me what not to do.

ED I taught him what my dad taught me, which is you can learn from everyone.

WOLFGANG That, and practice.

ED Actually he helped me more than I helped him.

WOLFGANG Yeah, I had to teach him how to play the songs again.

ED Because I couldn't remember the damn songs, and I don't know how to work a fuckin' iPod. He had one with all the songs on it. We hooked it up in the control room, and he'd go, "No dad, it goes like this!"

GW Did you teach yourself how to play the songs?

WOLFGANG Yeah, I did. The night before we started practicing, I sat down in my music room and I listened to every single song and just played to them. I didn't do exactly everything that's on the recordings. I put my own spin on it, but not enough to make people go, "Whoa, what's wrong with the bass?" I kept it as close as possible but added just a little...*spice*. A little WVH flair. [*laughs*]

GW Ed, What's it like to be onstage with your son as a band member, not just a special guest like he was on the previous tour?

ED It's an amazing feeling. I'm just so truly blessed. I have pictures of me sitting in the racquetball court in my pajamas with an acoustic guitar and Wolfgang is probably just two-and-a-half-feet tall. I'll never forget the day I saw his foot tapping along in beat! I knew then, I couldn't wait for the day I'd be able to make music with my son. I don't know what more I could ask for.

GW Even after playing about 40 shows together, do you still have moments?

ED Oh yeah. Every night. Sometimes we actually talk while we're playing. I'll go, "Hey! Are you all right?" because sometimes he'll look at me funny. When I give him a kiss or a high five or a low five, it's from the heart. It ain't bullshit. It's just pure love.

WOLFGANG That doesn't happen to me every night, but sometimes when I'm playing I'll forget to sing or play a certain note I'll look up and go, "Whoa, this is crazy!" That feeling is always there, but I don't always have time to think about it because I have a job to do.

ED I trip. You blow my mind. To be playing together is something I've always dreamed of. Believe it or not, I didn't know you'd be this good. He scares the shit out of me. He plays drums like a pro, too. The first thing he does in the house is start playing "And the Cradle Will Rock..." on the piano. Once Janie, my girlfriend, walked by and said, "Oh! I thought that was you." But it was Wolfie. Drums, guitar, bass, keyboards...shit! And singing!

GW What's it like to be in a band with your dad and uncle?

WOLFGANG It feels right.

ED That's the perfect way to put it. It just feels right.

WOLFGANG I don't ever go, "This is weird. I'm with a bunch of older people." I feel like we're all the same age. It's just what we do.

ED I was going to say the same thing. Every now and then when we're onstage playing, I'll look at him and go, God, that's my son! He's only 16, but he's not 16. He's an equal. Age doesn't matter.

WOLFGANG There's nobody else my age on the tour, but I feel like I'm an equal. I hope that everybody thinks of me the same way.

ED I believe they do, but you wouldn't believe the legalities we had to go through to have him be the bass player in Van Halen.

WOLFGANG I still have school.

GW Watching the band play onstage, it's like Wolfgang has been a member of this band for a long time. Why do you think you get along so well together?

WOLFGANG We're blood.

ED It's innately built-in. The way Wolfgang plays bass is very similar to the way I play guitar. It's very unorthodox. His style is interesting. When other bands come by, like Green Day, I'll go, "Close your eyes and listen to him." People freak out. [*Poison guitarist*] C.C. DeVille left me a message and he didn't compliment me at all. He did say I was on top of my game, but my son really impressed him. Do you know how proud that makes me? I couldn't ask for more. Not only has he proven himself but he also takes this stuff further. He does all the wicked shit on the bass that I do on guitar. It's fucking amazing.

WOLFGANG It's like a genetic metronome. When we end every song we don't even look at each other. We all feel it. It's all feel. It's good music and I love playing it.

GW Could you ever see yourself forming your own band and what would that band be like?

WOLFGANG I really have no idea. We'll just see what happens. I'm doing what I'm doing now.

ED If you do start your own band I'm going to be in it.

GW How are your friends reacting to your first job?

WOLFGANG My friends just see me as me. It's Wolfie. He's doing his thing.

ED But they must trip.

WOLFGANG They do. But they all really support me.

ED I'm sure they're proud of you.

GW What music do you listen to?

WOLFGANG Mainly rock stuff. Nothing too out of the ordinary. I really like Tool, which is one of my favorite bands, and I love Primus and Sevendust, too.

ED You were totally into AC/DC for a while.

WOLFGANG AC/DC is in all of our hearts because they rule.

ED You listen to us, too.

WOLFGANG Not any more. I haven't listened to us for a while.

ED That's because you're playing it now. I remember when I picked you up from school one day and there were boxes of records sitting in the shop at the studio. You looked at them and went, "Is this all you, dad?"

WOLFGANG Oh yeah. I probably was like five.

ED No, I think you were 10.

WOLFGANG Whatever.

ED It blew my mind that I totally forgot to turn him on to all the music that I've written. All he knew was what he heard on the radio.

WOLFGANG Like "Jump," and that was it.

ED I'll never forget when we were coming home from Castle Park [*a family entertainment center*]. "Hot for Teacher" came on the radio and Wolf was going, "Who is that singing?" I said, "That's Dave."

GW When did you start listening to your dad's recordings with David Lee Roth? What do you like about them?

WOLFGANG I'm not sure when I started.

ED You had to listen to them to learn them.

WOLFGANG Yeah, but I'm not sure when I started. I love it for the same reason everybody else loves it. It's awesome. It's just good music. It lasts. It was made a while ago, and it still lives today.

GW Van Halen music has never lost its adolescent appeal. For example, "Panama" was featured in the movie *Superbad*, and it fit perfectly even though the movie is set in the present day.

WOLFGANG I love that movie.

GW What is it about Van Halen music that makes it so timeless?

WOLFGANG It rocks.

ED It just lives and breathes. It's real. It's not contrived, premeditated or anything. It's just whatever comes out. If you try to write a song to please people and they don't like it, you're fucked because you're not pleasing yourself for one. And if they don't like it you're double fucked.

GW You write a lot of material. Do you have a gauge in your head that lets you know when something is ready to serve up to the table?

ED There's a lot of stuff I like that the rest of the guys don't. It's like that with "Panama." I rarely start on the one, and Al hears what I'm playing backward. I'll never forget when I wrote "Little Dreamer," which is one of the few where I do start on the one and he played backward to that too. Onstage when we're playing...

WOLFGANG ...Oh God, I have to watch you! At the end of "Unchained" we have to go eight or nine times before we freakin' end! Sometimes it's three. Sometimes it's five. It's always an odd number.

ED I can't count for some reason. It's always threes or fives for some reason. I only go by feel.

WOLFGANG And sometimes that feeling is wrong! [*laughs*] But we always somehow manage to pull it together for the ending.

ED We fall down the stairs and land on our feet together. Onstage, I look at Wolfie because he can count!

GW Has it always been that way, even before Wolfgang?

ED Yeah! But now I've got two people to help me, because both Al and Wolfie can count.

GW How do you approach your solo section every night?

ED There are certain things that I feel the fans really want to hear me play. "Eruption." "Cathedral."

WOLFGANG "Spanish Fly." The "Little Guitars" intro.

ED I noodle a bit. About the only complaint I get is that my solo is too long. Half the time I'm looking over at [*guitar tech*] Matt Bruck and going, Shit! Where do I go from here? Sometimes I don't know where to go because I forget all of the stuff that I've done. It's like what you asked me about why Van Halen's music has held up. It's because it's spontaneous and real. I'm not saying there's no thought behind it. Obviously it has to have some kind of structure. But spontaneity is the main ingredient.

GW Now that you've thoroughly road tested the EVH 5150 III amps, how do you feel they've improved or changed your tone?

ED It's just a natural progression. It's an extension of me, just like the guitar, which I named after my son even before he was in the band. The tattoo on my arm says it all.

GW You still use an old-school setup with a guitar cable and wedge monitors, and you control your own effects from an onstage pedal board. Why?

ED Because that's what I like. I don't like digital shit. My pedal board is homemade. It's all about sound. It's that simple. Wireless is wireless, and it's digital. Hopefully somewhere along the line somebody will add more ones to the zeros. When digital first started, I swear I could hear the gap between the ones and the zeros.

GW The wah-wah pedal is the newest addition to your rig.

ED It might appear that way to you, but I've used a wah since the early Nineties. I dig it, too. I use it more now than I ever have. I couldn't afford one back when we were starting out, but I always wanted one. The reason why I never used any kind of fuzz or distortion box is because I couldn't afford them.

GW What kind of wah are you using?

ED It's my own model made to my own specs by Dunlop. I just go by my ear and tell people this is how I want it to sound. A lot of people don't quite understand. Matt Bruck and I bust our asses to get people to understand what tone means. We're tone chasers, and until we get there we don't stop. That's what keeps us going.

GW You've brought a lot of different Wolfgang guitars on this tour, but you usually play one particular one at a show. However, at another show you may play another entirely different Wolfgang guitar that night. How do you choose which one you want to play that night?

ED The Wolfgang guitars I have are prototypes. I generally play the latest prototype. Hopefully it sounds better than the previous one, and if it does I end up playing it. I like the white one I'm playing better than the sunburst one, which I like better than the black ones.

GW Wolfgang, how did you choose your bass rig?

WOLFGANG Matt Bruck helped me a lot with the Sound City amps. When we were practicing Matt told me that he had these really cool amps, and we hooked them up. They rule.

ED Nobody gets a bass sound like he does. He uses EVH Brand 5150-III 4x12s. The same cabinets with EVH Celestion 12-inch speakers that I use.

WOLFGANG They're really out of the ordinary, but it works.

ED Everything starts here. [*Ed holds up Wolfgang's fingers.*]

WOLFGANG I split the signal between the amp and a DI, and I have a preamp as well. But the amp is the meat and potatoes of the sound.

GW Do you eventually see yourself having a solo segment onstage?

WOLFGANG I don't. I like having just my own moment for five seconds, like the "So This Is Love?" intro and doing the tapping part in "Romeo Delight." That's enough for me. It's like, Hey! Watch me play! I can do it! I'm more than fulfilled by being a team player.

GW What was your best personal moment so far on this tour?

WOLFGANG When we did the rehearsal show for our friends and family in L.A. It was just the beginning and I didn't feel I had ripened yet. When we came back to L.A. and did the first Staples Center show, I felt a sense of accomplishment. I was much a better player. I felt like a member of the band.

ED For me it's the fact that I get to play with my son, my brother and Dave. Every night is special. Doing an interview with my son right now is special. It's all special.

Lightning Source UK Ltd.
Milton Keynes UK
UKHW020815191222
414157UK00016B/1090